A Flower
Arranger's Garden

To my God-daughter,
Anne Savage,
who gave me the idea for the book

A Flower Arranger's Garden

Grizelda Maurice

B.T. BATSFORD LTD, LONDON

ISBN 0 7134 5373 7

Typeset by Tek-Art Ltd, Kent
and printed by
Anchor Brendon Ltd
Tiptree, Essex
for the publishers
B.T. Batsford Ltd
4 Fitzhardinge Street
London W1H 0AH

Contents

Acknowledgements

My very grateful thanks are due to all those who helped me in preparing this book. The illustrations are a vital part of it, and I am immensely indebted to Mrs Shelagh Collingwood, who not only took beautiful photographs but also was constantly ready with ideas and advice. Once again I am extremely grateful to Mr Bruce Hyatt, for his charming and meticulous line drawings which are invaluable in illustrating the text. I also thank Mrs Joy Saunders, who helped me greatly in my research.

I thank my publishers, and especially Miss Rachel Wright, for much help and advice, and Mrs Wendy Morgan for typing many of the lists of plants. Above all I thank my husband for typing the rest of the manuscript and for the help and encouragement which he has given me in many ways.

G.M.

Introduction

My god-daughter is entirely responsible for my writing this book. We were looking at her new garden and discussing her plans for it. 'I love arranging flowers and I love gardening,' she said, 'but somehow the two don't seem to come together. Why don't you write a book called A *Flower Arranger's Garden*? That would help people like me to combine our two interests.' I was very taken with her idea, because from my own experience and comments from flower arranger friends I felt that she had hit on a real need.

It seemed to me that the book should be primarily for the owners of small gardens, partly because I could then write from my own experience, and partly because in large gardens there is really no problem as areas can be set aside for cutting beds. In a small garden, however, material for cutting has to be found from the flowers and shrubs which are also part of the general design.

I am ashamed to say that for many years our small garden was very neglected. I think that my defeatist attitude was influenced by memories of a childhood spent in Guernsey. There we had a lovely garden, in late winter filled with camellias and spring flowers, and in summer – in retrospect seemingly always hot – full of colour and delight, due entirely to my father, who was a passionate gardener. In contrast our small patch seemed very uninspiring.

This attitude was very foolish. As a professional florist and decorator it is essential for me to have interesting flowers and foliage and I realized that our garden could provide exactly that if we used our space imaginatively. We found after a time that we had in fact the basis of a very pretty garden. It includes brick, flint walls and paths and the cottage itself is seventeenth century – the whole making a good background for shrubs and climbing plants.

The garden soil started off as pretty heavy Hertfordshire clay, but over the years it has been improved and lightened by good garden compost and other appropriate fertilizers. Clearly the planting of any garden is dependent on such matters as soil and aspect, and unless plants are to be kept solely in containers certain limitations have to be faced. Therefore, we decided to keep to indigenous plants as far as possible, but to make full use of peat when this was needed. Our aim was to include a variety of good evergreen shrubs, climbers, interesting coloured foliage and berried plants as well as a wide collection of herbaceous flowers. We utilized every nook and cranny: a damp corner was turned into a mini-fernery, and ground cover was used for pretty leaves. There is a wide variety of bulbs and so on from tiny cyclamens to large Crown Imperials.

At first our gardening knowledge was non-existent, but over the years we have learned by trial and error and of course are still learning what succeeds and what fails. One of the things which we have discovered is the importance of correct colour grouping. This is something that applies both to the garden and when arranging flowers, so I have gone into this topic in some detail.

I have also learned how the garden can provide my flower arranging activities with a continual source of interesting plant material. Actually I hate the term 'flower arranger' – it sounds tremendously high powered – but I mean by the term those of us who enjoy arranging flowers, whether it is a large group or a tiny vase of mixed leaves and flowers. Nothing is more satisfactory than to walk in the garden on a winter's day and suddenly come across some half-hidden teasure to cut and bring indoors.

Because I am concerned with arranging as much as with growing I have concentrated on material which I know from experience will last reasonably well in water or Oasis. In the chapter on conditioning you will find that modern methods have helped to extend the life of flowers which a few years ago would have been useless to the flower arranger. However, there are still some which will not last in water under any conditions, so these I have omitted.

In the chapter on flowers for special occasions I have resisted the temptation to suggest combining hot-house or imported flowers, keeping to material which can be grown in your garden. Nevertheless, the scope is still wide and I hope that this book will extend the reader's range of decorating. The chapter on dried materials explains how seed heads and many flowers can be preserved either to be used on their own or mixed with fresh cut flowers and foliage and thus provide a further source of supply.

The gardeners have been wonderfully served with a never-ending stream of books and television programmes; indeed, I have been very grateful for many of them myself. I think, however, that flower arrangers who want help in planning their gardens specifically to meet their needs have been neglected, and I hope that this book will fill the gap.

1. Planning the garden

As appears from the introduction, the aim of this book is to help flower arrangers plan their gardens so that the planting will at all times include a wide range of cutting material. This means not only a selection of different flowers but, even more important, different coloured foliage plants, berries and seed heads – all the varied colours and textures which go to make interesting groups for the house or church. It is necessary, however, to consider not only cut material – if that were the case an allotment could meet the need – but how to plan an interesting garden. However small the area it is perfectly possible to achieve the two aims. I must stress that the flower arranger is not concerned solely with large groups: equally important are small posies containing special treasures which as the year advances become particularly valuable. Coloured leaves or late berries in November give just as much pleasure as an armful of summer flowers.

It is possible to learn a great deal from other people's gardens. I do suggest that you visit these armed with a notebook: before I was more organized I used to jot down plant names on anything that came to hand, ending with a hideous day of reckoning when I wanted some special piece of information! In Britain we are fortunate because not only are there large gardens regularly open to the public but from time to time there is also the chance of seeing small gardens to which visitors are admitted at certain weekends in aid of charity. It is by visiting gardens large and small that I have come to understand about design – what colours look good together and how plants or shrubs can be used to achieve the right combination of shape, form and texture.

Many large gardens are in fact often a series of little gardens, leading from one to another, sometimes each different in colour. The brilliant garden at Hidcote, designed by Colonel Johnstone, and Sissinghurst, created by Harold Nicholson and his wife Vita Sackville West, are two good examples. Both of them are now managed beautifully by The National Trust. Often a corner or part of a bed in a large garden can spark off ideas for a small one. Particular backgrounds, such as brick or stone walls or special hedging, provide inspiration for the new gardener.

A fount of information, particularly of a specialized kind, is the Royal Horticultural Society's garden at Wisley. Members of the society are, moreover, able to go to lectures which are invaluable. There are also the Society's Halls in Vincent Square in London which have shows throughout the year. They are small and as yet not too crowded, so that the exhibitors can spare time to answer questions and talk about the plants on view, which are beautifully staged. The spring planting is particularly good – the woodland gardens are most imaginatively set out – and provides an opportunity to learn about new plants. For example, my knowledge of early coloured primroses and unusual shade-loving plants is entirely due to these shows.

If you are planning a new garden you must study the site at different times of the day. Observe first of all when and where the shade will be greatest. A slanting roof line or a neighbour's wall or tree can throw surprisingly long shadows. Remember that a bare winter tree is very different in high summer. My family find it incomprehensible that I never know which way a house faces – or indeed whether I am driving east or west. So for fellow sufferers may I suggest that they clarify their compass points from the start! It took me some time to work out that a south wall means the side of the wall which faces south, so the other side is north-facing, and so on. Correct orientation is particularly essential when it comes to planning beds and planting tender shrubs

It is also important to take note at an early stage of the garden's advantages and disadvantages. An ugly, ragged wall may need trellis and climbers to hide it. On the other hand, an attractive brick or stone wall needs plants which will enhance its texture and outline. Make full use of trees and other features. In our garden we have a *Clematis montana* climbing up an old apple tree, itself under-planted with spring bulbs which grow through good coloured ground cover and small ivies. The adjoining beds, shaded by the tree, are full of hellebores, polyanthus, euphorbia and alchemilla, flanked by a hedge of syringa, symphoricarpus and skimmia, and lightened by legustrum, ilex and acuba. Note that many plants thrive in the shade, provided that they have air, but too many overhanging trees will very much limit growth. An area shaded by a tall viburnum and dampened by the dripping of a rainwater butt has been planted with ferns, special primulas, primroses, *Arum italicum*, hostas and various pulmonaria.

Square trellis may be used not only to cover shabby walls but also as a barrier, provided that it is well covered with climbers and wall shrubs. If more privacy is needed, use a good closely-boarded wooden fencing. The prettiest boundaries are, of course, old brick and stone walls, but they are expensive. If the garden is small it is unwise to make the boundary walls too high, because the higher they are the more shade you get.

A garden is far more interesting if there are different levels – for example, a terrace leading down to a lawn and beds. We have a small raised rockery with special plants backed by an old chimney pot filled with trailing ivies and vinca, together with a clematis. Even in a small garden vistas and surprises can be created. For example, in our garden a path of old brick leads between two tallish chimney pots filled with cascading plants on to a flint boundary wall, against which a brick trough is planted with *Hydrangea petiolaris* scrambling up the wall, hostas, ivies and other trailing plants completing the vista.

Once note has been taken of the essential features of the garden, the all-important positioning of flower beds can be planned. The shape of a bed is very much a matter of personal taste. Ours is a cottage garden, so very straight, formal beds would be unsympathetic. We prefer the beds to be slightly curved and for plants to tumble over the edges.

Soils vary enormously. In our village there is a great variation from one garden to the next. There are good soil kits to help to pinpoint the sort of soil to be found in each part of your garden. In our shady area we have dug in a great deal of peat to encourage peat-loving plants. In a small garden it is wise to concentrate on indigenous plants which like your local soil, or which can be grown in large pots containing the right mixture, rather than to import special soil which has to be added to constantly. We manage to keep a bin of compost going, but I do augment it with a steady watering of phostrogen throughout the summer.

In a small garden there is not much room for trees so very careful thought is needed when choosing them. They should be chosen for shape and colour. A weeping tree, like *Pyrus salicifolia pendula*, which has silvery grey foliage arching down to the ground and little white flowers in April, makes an interesting feature. Syringa, philadelphus and similar strong flowering trees are in a small garden best kept as part of a hedge or against a wall.

Before bedding plants are chosen climbers and wall shrubs should be put in because they provide a background to the whole scheme. If there are already

1 Basket of spring flowers, ferns and fatshedera leaf

established climbing plants and shrubs, additions should be complementary to them, with carefully blending colours. When choosing new plants take account of the background which they are to have. Wooden fencing and stone walls are complimentary to all colours, but dominant colour-washes and orange bricks, often found in house walls, are very unbecoming to certain pinks and reds. Paler colours, such as creams and some yellows, provide a more sympathetic contrast, and make a definite contribution to the garden scheme. Be careful that you have enough contrast – a white climber against a white wall may become quite lost.

Before choosing plants do make sure that your site will meet the plants' particular needs. Remember that if the climate is a harsh one tender plants may not survive the winter. It is so easy to get carried away by a garden centre or someone else's garden where the soil, situation and climate are quite different. Some plants must have a south-facing wall, some must have shade or partial shade, other thrive on that difficult north-facing wall.

So do not, I beg you, make the mistakes which I have made in the past: they are very expensive and frustrating. Buy from a reputable source and be quite sure that you get proper advice. Most garden centres and nurseries have at least one reliable and knowledgeable person, so do not hesitate to ask questions. The less reputable nurseries are very irresponsible and vow that a tender plant will weather the bleakest climate when quite clearly it will do nothing of the sort. There are, of course, other sources. Many coffee mornings include plant stalls, as do many gardens open to the public, and these are a fount of treasures; likewise friends' gardens. I find myself calling the plants after the friends who have given them to me – that can be confusing.

If possible climbers and shrubs are best planted in the spring, especially if they are at all tender. Then they have a chance to establish themselves before the next winter. Climbing plants need to be planted at least one foot away from a wall or fence with supporting canes bending back towards it. Climbers and shrubs and of course trees need a lot of water when first planted and until they are well established. A wall takes away a lot of moisture. Some plants near to walls are particularly vulnerable to drought.

Once the chosen trees and shrubs have been positioned, the rest of the planting can take place, using the background as a guide to colour schemes. Flower arrangers know that to create a successful group there must be a mixture of colour, form and texture: the gardener uses plant material in the same way. A garden needs careful colour planning and careful use of different contrasting materials. It needs both architectural plants – those with clear lines like phormium, yucca and Iris variegata – and on the other hand plants of irregular shape, including some which flow naturally over the edge of the bed, like nepeta, violas and dianthus.

Light shrubs should be used to contrast with dark ones. For example, to lighten the effect of a dark corner planted with mahonia and a very tall double philadelphus, both of which have limited flowering seasons, we have a variegated weigela, a tall grey *Eucalyptus gunnii*, and a small grey *Salix helvetica*, together with tubs and urns staged at different levels and filled with lilies, geraniums, helichrysum and mixed ivies. All these containers are moved from time to time as the contents cease flowering. One bed is flanked with shrubs and climbers and contains mostly different coloured foliage plants. Another is massed with plants, with barely any earth to be seen. We aim to have deeper reds and pinks in the centre, fading out to pale colours mixed with white. To achieve this effect one must know roughly at what seasons flowers will bloom so that they can be grouped to come out together. Use shrubs and ground cover for further contrast.

We have some lilies in the beds, but they are kept in pots sunk into the earth as otherwise they disappear. (Mice perhaps?) The beds are underplanted in front with small spring bulbs, such as miniature narcissus, snowdrops, crocuses and grape hyacinths.

It is not possible to discuss every flower or plant which may be useful to the flower arranger, but in the lists which follow I include those which seem to me to be the most important, dividing them into nine sections, as follows:

1. Shrubs
2. Climbers
3. Herbaceous
4. Bulbs, corms, tubers and rhizomes
5. Ground cover
6. Shade-loving plants
7. Grasses and grass-like plants
8. Ferns
9. Grey plants

I have chosen shrubs not only for their flowers but also for their foliage and berries and I have listed separately the more obvious climbers for the sake of easy identification.

I have then discussed suitable material colour by colour and go on to discuss colour grouping. It is impossible to plan a colour scheme for the garden unless one knows what colours are available: often a carefully planned scheme falls apart because of mistiming of the flowering season. There then follow tables in which the material covered by sections one to four is listed by reference to both colour and time of flowering, so that the reader may, for example, discover what pink flowering shrubs are available in summer.

As this is not primarily a gardening book, I have not attempted when listing shrubs etc., to give full growing instructions but have merely mentioned habitat and discussed methods of conditioning. There is a separate chapter on the subject of conditioning.

The patio garden

By patio garden I mean a small paved area such as is often found in front of or at the back of a town house. It may be possible to construct one or two small raised beds, but most growing will have to be confined to containers. In one way this is an advantage, as each shrub or plant can be given its own particular soil: but remember that soil becomes exhausted and needs feeding or renewal.

What I have said about aspect is of particular importance in a small space largely enclosed by buildings, where sunlight is at a premium. Nevertheless, there are many shrubs in the lists at the end of this chapter which will thrive in such a position, and the very fact that it is more sheltered than the average garden makes it possible to grow tender varieties which might not survive elsewhere. There are some plants, such as geraniums and helichrysum, which cannot be left out all winter. They can be taken out, brought into the house, and replaced by spring bulbs. Troughs planted with miniature narcissus, *Iris reticulata* and muscari make an attractive feature. Bulbs should also include a wide variety of different lilies. They will then flower over a long season.

Climbers, such as clematis, honeysuckle and perpetual flowering roses, do very well in containers and are particularly suitable for a patio garden surrounded by high walls. There are many attractive species of ivy which love the shade.

No matter how small the area it can be made very attractive by the use of containers at different levels, including hanging baskets and window-boxes, perhaps planted with ivies, helichrysum, verbena and similar trailing plants.

Some houses have steps leading down to a dampish basement area. I have seen a very successful fernery created in these conditions. The steps were used as an ascending staging for pot plants at every level. These were limited to cream and pale pink fuchsias and ivy-leaf geraniums with variegated leaves – very cool and attractive. Planning should take account of permanent features. For example, a large earthenware pot might be planted so as to carry out the colour-scheme of a climbing rose. Lilies do well in pots and can be brought into the house for special occasions.

To ensure that there is plenty of interest throughout the year care must be taken to choose material which has a long flowering season, and also good evergreen shrubs, particularly those giving a variety of colouring, such as eleagnus and euonymus, which contrast well with the glossy dark foliage of camellia and fatsia. An architectural shrub, like phormium with its striped ribbon-like leaves, adds further interest. It is a good idea to add berried shrubs like pyracanthus and skimmia for the autumn.

Even within the limits of a patio garden there will be material for cutting. In a raised bed there can, for example, be dianthus, campanula, nicotiana (which, incidentally, smells lovely at night) and some interesting foliage plants like hosta and bergenia, while the shrubs will also provide a varied selection of leaves and berries.

Shrubs

Arundinaria (bamboo)
Useful for many flower arrangements either as backing for a tall group, or as a source of long, ribbon-like leaves used separately for their shape and colour. They last well in water.

A. *variegata*: medium sized, has pretty variegated leaves. Spreads quickly.

A. *viridistriata*: hardy small plant with attractive narrow green leaves striped with yellow – some leaves are pure yellow.

HABITAT: will grow in most well-drained soils.

CONDITIONING: cut stems and give long drink after boiling vinegar treatment.

Aucuba
A. *japonica*: a useful evergreen with bright green leaves with yellow markings. It looks well in a dark corner in the garden and makes interesting foliage for large groups.

'Golden Spangles': a good variety.

HABITAT: in any soil and sun or shade.

CONDITIONING: split ends and give long drink.

Berberis
An evergreen and deciduous shrub with about 60 different varieties, some of which have brilliant autumn colouring and berries. It is very prickly to cut but worth the effort.

B. *darwinii*: evergreen about six ft with small holly-like leaves. In May it has clusters of orange flowers and in autumn brilliantly-coloured foliage and superb plum-coloured fruits.

B. × *stenophylla*: good arching stems bearing coral berries in autumn.

B. *thunbergii* 'Atropurpurea Nana': dwarf, pink foliage in autumn.

HABITAT: any well-drained soil.

CONDITIONING: split ends, long drink.

Buxus (box)
The ordinary box (B*uxus sempervirens*) is a rather dull evergreen but there are more interesting variegated varieties that last very well in water and make an attractive backing for garlands.

B. *sempervirens aureovariegata*: medium size evergreen. The leaves are splashed with cream. It likes to be pruned, so is excellent for flower arrangers.

B. *sempervirens elegantissima*: slow growing with small grey-green leaves edged with cream.

HABITAT: well-drained soils.

CONDITIONING: hammer ends and give long drink. It lasts very well in water and will for special occasions last some hours out of water.

Camellia

Camellia provides evergreen glossy foliage that lasts up to five weeks when cut, and in late winter and early spring the branches are covered with single or double rose-like blooms varying in colour from white to pale/deep pink and red. I love branches arranged on their own, or as part of a mixed spring group. One or two sprays cut while the flowers are in bud will last for several weeks and the flowers will open naturally. The flowers are easily bruised so if you are taking camellia to arrange in a church or some distance away, make sure the flowers are protected.

The two hardy varieties are C. *japonica* and C. × *williamsii*. C × *williamsii* is the larger of the two and has the advantage that as the flowers fade they fall to the ground and are replaced by more blooms. C. *japonica* holds on to the dead flowers.

There are endless cultivars and it is very hard to pick out special varieties.
C. *japonica* 'Adolphe Audusson': an old, well-tried plant, hardy and free flowering. Impressive large semi-double blood-red flowers.
C. *japonica* 'Ama-no-Kawa': an attractive white, single flower which is popular with flower arrangers.
C. *japonica* 'Elegans': large deep-pink anemone-type flowers.
C × *williamsii* 'Donation': has become very popular. It flowers freely and has good soft-pink semi-double flowers – mine produced a mass of flowers the second year of planting.
HABITAT: camellia does not like chalky soils but flourishes in a good acid or neutral peaty soil. Needs to be protected from early morning sun and searing wind, and must have its roots in shade. Flourishes in shady woodland areas. A good feed of mulch is essential and two or three liquid feeds in the autumn when the buds are forming.
CONDITIONING: hammer ends. Long drink. Pick in bud, which will open naturally.

Caryopteris

The splendid little dwarf shrub C. *clandonensis* bears deep blue flowers from September to the end of October – I like it mixed with other autumn flowers and berries.
C. *clandonensis* 'Arthur Simmonds': dwarf and compact. It has bright-blue flowers and small grey-green leaves.
C. *clandonensis* 'Kew Blue': deeper blue flowers.
HABITAT: well-drained soil in a sunny position. Best in front of a sunny border.
CONDITIONING: split ends and give a long warm drink.

Ceratostigma

An enchanting plant bearing bright, clear-blue flowers.
C. *willmottianum*: reddish leaves in the autumn – the flowers bloom from mid-

summer to October. The combination of red leaves and blue flowers makes it a unique shrub.

HABITAT: normally ceratostigma only reaches 18 in. but if planted against a warm wall it may reach three ft. Any soil including chalk.

CONDITIONING: boiling water treatment.

Chaenomeles (ornamental quince)

This is a deciduous shrub or wall plant. In a small garden this shrub is better trained against walls, otherwise it grows too large. It is useful for flower arrangers, having long slender stems covered in pale-green small leaves and clusters of cup-shaped flowers varying in colour from white to peachy-pink and orangey-red. It flowers from January to June although I have had flowers at Christmas.

C. *speciosa* 'Moerloosei': pale pink and white flowers.

C. *speciosa* 'Nivalis': pure white flowers.

HABITAT: sunny position and well-drained soil.

CONDITIONING: hammer ends. Long drink.

Choisya

C. *ternata*: another favourite evergreen shrub. Useful shiny-green foliage, which lasts well when cut, and in May the shrub bears clusters of white star-like flowers which are scented. I used it in the mock standard trees described on page 117 and also find it a marvellous addition to large groups for both the foliage and the flowers.

HABITAT: well-drained soil in any sunny position. Feed it at the end of its flowering season to ensure that it will flower again in September.

CONDITIONING: hammer ends, long drink, especially if the stems have flowers.

Cornus (dogwood)

The foliage is unreliable if it is required to last for any length of time. However carefully conditioned one or two branches seem to droop for no apparent reason, but I include it in A *Flower Arranger's Garden* because some varieties have coloured bark – a stem or two for a winter vase is invaluable. Some of the shrubs have brilliant red bark, some yellow.

C. *alba* 'Elegantissima': an exceptional variety with soft-grey-green leaves margined creamy-white and red bark.

C. *kousa chinensis*: a quite exceptional shrub. In May and June it produces tiny flowers surrounded by large white bracts which last well when cut and in the autumn red leaves which dry well by the carpet method (see page 100).

HABITAT: a rampant grower in most soils. C. *kousa chinensis* requires some peat or leafmould dug into the soil.

CONDITIONING: some foliage branches will last with boiling water treatment and very long drink.

Corylopsis

This is a very special deciduous flowering shrub and has delicate slim arching sprays covered with pale yellow spikes.

C. *spicata*: my favourite as it appears in February, which is a great joy.

C. *willmottiae*: flowers later in March and April.

HABITAT: ordinary garden soil in full sun. It prefers moderately-rich loamy soil. It is tender so needs a sheltered position in cold areas.

CONDITIONING: split ends very carefully and give long drink in warm water.

Corylus (hazel)

Flower arrangers need unusual material to make interesting groups and Corylus has some excellent types.

C. *avellana* 'Contorta': one of the most spectacular with pale-lemon-yellow tassel-like catkins hanging down from twisted, contorted stems. I like them arranged in a tall vase on their own or impaled by a pin holder on a flat dish. The shape of the branches then stands out well. Even when the catkins have fallen, the furiously-twisted stems make an interesting feature.

HABITAT: any well-drained soil. Will tolerate some shade.

CONDITIONING: hammer ends. Long drink.

Cotoneaster

An evergreen and deciduous shrub which is invaluable to the flower arranger. The shrubs vary very much in size from a prostrate form which comes under the heading of ground cover to large spreading bushes. The leaves are dark green and many varieties have splendid arching stems, weighted down with red or yellow berries in the autumn. The small flowers which appear in spring are of no real interest.

C. × *hybridus pendulus*: easy to train up against a wall in which case there will be cascading branches bearing bright-red fruits in the autumn.

'John Waterer': an elegant evergreen or semi-evergreen shrub growing up to ten ft high. The cascading branches bear willow-like leaves and clusters of scarlet fruits in autumn.

C. *serotinus*: small evergreen leaves and in the autumn dense bunches of bright-red berries which will stay until the new year.

HABITAT: any well-drained soil, sun or shade.

CONDITIONING: hammer ends and give long drink.

Cytisus (broom)

Any shrub that flourishes on poor soil is an advantage to many gardens and cytisus does just that. It has cascading slender stems covered with tiny pea-like flowers.

C. × *praecox*: one of the best. The stems are covered with yellow or white flowers from April to May.

HABITAT: thrives on well-drained soil in a sunny position but tolerates sandy and peaty soil.

CONDITIONING: boiling water treatment and long deep drink.

Daphne

This group includes deciduous and evergreen shrubs, some of which flower in winter and early spring.

D. *mezereum*: deciduous and hardy. Bears rosy-purple or white flowers in February and red or yellow berries in autumn.

HABITAT: any soil, any situation.

CONDITIONING: hammer ends, boiling water treatment, very long drink.

D. *odora 'Aureomarginata'*: this is the best variety in my opinion. The leaves are evergreen and margined with cream. Slender stems bear pale-pink, scented flowers in March.

HABITAT: needs good moisture retentive soil. Dig in peat and leafmould before planting in sunny position.

CONDITIONING: boiling water treatment and at least six hours in deep water.

Deutzia

This is particularly suitable for large groups arranged for summer weddings. Its cascading stems are covered with either white or pink small flowers.

D. *gracilis*: small variety with white flowers.

D. *gracilis 'Perle Rose'*: pale-pink flowers in June.

HABITAT: any good well-drained soil and a sunny position.

CONDITIONING: boiling water treatment, long drink.

Elaeagnus

A most popular evergreen shrub. The foliage is bright-green with yellow markings; it is a good addition in the garden as it lights up dark corners.

E. *pungens 'Aurea'*: leaves margined in bright yellow.

C. *pungens 'Dicksonii'*: wider golden margin. Some leaves are indeed yellow which makes it particularly good for an all yellow group. It is very slow growing, so suitable for small gardens.

E. *pungens 'Maculata'*: the richest colouring of all. It has bright-yellow marked leaves and it too is slow growing.

HABITAT: in any well-drained soil and sunny position. Like all variegated shrubs, it is likely to revert to green. Stems which revert must be removed at point of origin.

CONDITIONING: hammer stems and give long drink.

Erica

These useful low-growing evergreen shrubs are known to most of us as heather. They provide the flower arranger with attractive spiky stems covered with tiny flowers ranging from pink to white and mauve. Many of them have coloured stems and leaves. They start flowering in winter so mix well with hellebores and early spring flowers.

E. *calluna argentea*: silvery leaves.

E. *calluna vulgaris*: the single species of the genus, more commonly known as ling heather.

E. *calluna vulgaris 'Sealei' aurea*: has golden leaves and white flowers.

E. *carnea*: rosy-purple flowers from December to April.

E. *carnea 'Eileen Pouter'*: carmine flowers in October.

E. *vivellii*: smaller shrubs in shades of pink, carmine and white. They flower from October onward.

HABITAT: Erica needs lime free soil and a sunny position. There are some ericas that will grow on any soil and are less low-growing reaching up to one ft which make them a useful cut flower.

CONDITIONING: snip ends and long drink. Some stems will dry off quite naturally if left in a vase.

Escallonia

It surprises me that this useful flowering shrub with arching stems covered in small, dark, evergreen leaves and bearing a profusion of tiny pink-red or white flowers is not used more often. There are several good varieties:

'Apple-Blossom': pale-pink flowers.

'Donard Brilliance': deeper-pink flowers.

'Edinensis': arching stems with clear, pink flowers.

'Slieve Donard': compact medium-sized shrub with white flushed pink flowers in June.

In many seaside gardens *Escallonia macrantha* abounds – pretty, rosy-red flowers. It flourishes less well inland as it is inclined to suffer frost damage. It is often used as a hedging shrub in seaside areas, in which case it provides useful small sprays for posies and garlands.

HABITAT: good soil and sunny position.

CONDITIONING: hammer ends and long drink.

Eucryphia

This is larger than most shrubs chosen for A *Flower Arranger's Garden*. I have included it because it is a superb garden and flower arranger's shrub. It is unsuitable for a very small garden. In late summer and early autumn it is covered with pure-white flowers resembling Philadelphus.

E. *glutinosa*: a deciduous shrub which may reach ten ft. Large, scented, white single flowers with prominent stamens. The leaves turn yellow and red in autumn.

E. 'Rostrevor': small evergreen tree, slender upright-growing branches, covered in fragrant, white, cup-like flowers in August and September.

HABITAT: moist, lime-free soil.

CONDITIONING: the flowers last better if most of the leaves are removed. Boiling water treatment and long drink.

Eunoymus

A very useful evergreen shrub much loved by flower arrangers. It is slow-growing except for the climbing varieties like E. *Fortunei radicans* which cling to walls and fences. A south-facing, warm brick wall encourages quick growth and provides long slender stems of pretty variegated leaves which are particularly useful for winter groups.

E. *europaeus* (*spindle tree*): a useful deciduous berried shrub.

'*Red Cascade*': particularly good as the arching stems are weighted down by clusters of dark red fruits.

HABITAT: grows well in chalk or lime.

CONDITIONING: hammer ends well and give long drink.

E. *fortunei* '*Emerald 'n Gold*': one of the best variegated shrubs, bright-yellow and green leaves with a pink tinge in winter.

E. *fortunei* '*Silver Queen*': pretty creamy-yellow leaves in spring, becoming green with creamy-white margins.

HABITAT: any good soil. Will tolerate sun or shade.

CONDITIONING: hammer stems, otherwise no special treatment, but resist picking the immature spring foliage as it does not last well in water.

Euphorbia

There are many marvellous varieties that are invaluable, providing interesting cut material for a long season.

E. *amygdaloides* '*Purpurea*': one of the most interesting. Maroon stems, dark evergreen leaves. New spring shoots are bright red.

E. *griffithii* '*Fireglow*': small, flat, apricot-red heads and bright-green foliage from June to August.

E. *myrsinites*: unusual, waxy, blue leaves bearing large heads of limey-green flowers tinged with apricot – early spring.

E. *polychroma* (E. *Epithymoides*): mounds of brassy-yellow heads all spring that are superb for mixed green groups. It is a very dominant colour in a small garden.

E. *robbiae*: tall rosettes of dark green foliage and later pretty heads of yellow-green flowers – also a good flower for green groups.

E. *wulfenii*: does well in a dry garden. Long, brown, stiff stems with good blue-grey foliage. In March and April each stem carries large heads of lime-green disc-like flowers.

HABITAT: most varieties will grow easily in any well-drained soil. E. *wulfenii*, however, needs protection from winds.

CONDITIONING: boiling water treatment is essential and then a long drink.

The plant exudes a white substance which can be poisonous – so be warned.

Fatsia

One of the best evergreen shrubs is F*atsia japonica*. The main stout stems break into slimmer stalks bearing huge, shining leaves looking like large, green hands. In early winter it bears clusters of tiny cream-coloured flowers. The leaves are useful in mixed green groups or as a strong contrast to autumn flower arrangements.

F. *japonica* 'Variegata': less hardy. The lobed leaves are bordered with white at the tips and margins.

HABITAT: sun or shady situation is possible but Fatsia prefers a sheltered spot. Looks well against walls.

CONDITIONING: split ends and long drink.

Forsythia

Yellow flowering shrub that mixes in well with spring flowers. There are several varieties. I avoid the very bright yellow as I find it overpowering in a small garden.

F. *suspensa*: a weeping deciduous variety. The arching stems are covered with pale-yellow flowers.

F.S. 'Atrocaulis': decorative purple stems, pale-lemon-yellow flowers from March to April.

HABITAT: against any wall or fence.

CONDITIONING: hammer ends, long drink. If you wish to force it open in February, cut and place in a deep bucket in a warm room. It will take about three weeks.

Fuchsia

There are many attractive varieties, some of which are hardy. The arching stems bearing flowers often with a deeper coloured corolla, backed by paler sepals, make it a decorative shrub. The colours vary from white and pale-pink to red and mixed mauve and pink. The magellanica varieties flower from June to October and may reach a height of six ft in sheltered areas. Among the many varieties are:

F. *magellanica* 'Gracilis': graceful slender stems bearing a profusion of small scarlet and purple flowers.

F. *magellanica* 'Variegata': green leaves flushed creamy-white and pink. Attractive plant for summer borders and excellent foliage for flower arrangements.

F. *magellanica* 'Versicolor': particularly decorative shrub with superb silvery-grey leaves margined with creamy-white and pink centres. I use it in mixed summer vases.

'Phyllis': an old fashioned variety seen in many gardens. Its arching stems bearing red flowers are particularly good in a clashing red group or on their own with grey or variegated foliage.

HABITAT: all fuchsias should be planted a few inches below ground level and if the garden is in an exposed area the roots should be protected in winter by peat.

CONDITIONING: boiling water treatment and then a long drink in tepid water.

Garrya

G. *elliptica*: this shrub is sometimes known as the silk-tassel bush which describes exactly its exotic, long silvery-green catkins. It is an interesting evergreen shrub. The catkins are born on male plants. It has greyish leaves and mixes well with all green groups or with yellow flowering shrubs like winter jasmin. The catkins appear in November and are in evidence up to the end of February.

HABITAT: flourishes on poor soils as well as chalk or in seaside areas. It will tolerate shade.

CONDITIONING: slit ends and long drink.

Griselinia

A very attractive, rather tender, evergreen shrub.

G. 'littoralis variegata': the best variety for flower arrangers. Pale-green, oval, shiny leaves with golden margins that fade with age.

HABITAT: mild areas, flourishes in seaside gardens.

CONDITIONING: slit ends and long drink.

Hamamelis mollis (witch hazel)

An unusual slow growing shrub. The bare stems are covered with yellow tassel-like flowers from early January. One or two stems cut for the house are a great joy. The large hazel-like leaves turn yellow in the autumn.

HABITAT: any well-drained soil and situation. They show up well against evergreen shrubs.

CONDITIONING: slit stems, long drink.

Hebe

Good evergreen shrub sometimes known as Veronica. There are many varieties and it is a useful provider of small, lasting foliage for mixed posies.

H. *andersonii* 'Variegata': has handsome broad leaves edged in creamy-white and can reach four to five ft.

HABITAT: will grow anywhere including chalk.
CONDITIONING: slit ends and good drink.

Hydrangea
These are useful shrubs because the flower heads can be dried for winter arrangements. They also provide attractive large flowers in white, pink and in some varieties a spectacular blue for autumn groups. 'Lace-cap' hydrangea are my favourite. Large flat heads with small dense flowers in the middle with larger looser ones at the edge. 'Blue wave' is superb. 'Lamarth white' is suitable for use in wedding groups.

H. *paniculata grandiflora*: attractive cone-shaped spikes of white flowers on long arching stems.
HABITAT: moisture retentive soil is essential, otherwise it will droop in hot weather. I have to water mine very regularly.
CONDITIONING: slit the stems and boiling water treatment followed by soaking for several hours. Spray the heads regularly if they are arranged in a large group.

Ilex (holly)
The only holly that I would plant in a small garden is a variegated one.
I. *altaclarensis*: 'Golden King': excellent. I use it all the year round as it has smooth-edged leaves with a decorative gold edge.
I. *crenata* 'Golden Gem': a small shrub with pretty yellow leaves. It stands out well in bare winter gardens and provides interesting cut foliage.
HABITAT: most garden soils and tolerates some shade.
CONDITIONING: slit ends and short drink.

Kerria
K. *japonica* 'Pleniflora': has long arching stems bearing tiny yellow rose-like flowers in April and May. It mixes well with spring flowers.
HABITAT: needs well drained soil. Any position.
CONDITIONING: slit ends and long drink.

Kolkwitzia
K. *amabilis* (*beauty bush*): in May and June this shrub produces arching sprays covered in small bell-like flowers in soft pink tinged with yellow. It mixes well in any summer group; later in the season there are good seed heads.
'Pink Cloud': an excellent variety, with profuse deeper-pink flowers.
HABITAT: very hardy. It will thrive in any soil but prefers a sunny position.
CONDITIONING: boiling water treatment and then a long drink in cold water.

Leycesteria
L. *formosa*: a hardy deciduous, quick growing shrub. In July and August white flowers form long pendulous tassels – these are overlapped by maroon bracts. I like to remove some of the leaves and arrange stems in a tall white vase.

However, a choice has to be made. If the flowers remain on the bush they will be followed by beautiful black berries which look marvellous arranged with bright red autumn flowers – so take your choice as you cannot have both!

HABITAT: like a good rich soil in sun. It will tolerate chalky and clay soil and shade.

CONDITIONING: hammer ends and give boiling water treatment and long drink.

Ligustrum (golden privet)

This is a semi-evergreen shrub. In a small garden the golden variety is the most useful. Its bright-yellow leaves stand out well as a foil to dark colours. It provides the flower arranger with long stems covered in small yellow-edged leaves, and lasts well in water.

'Aureum': the best variety.

HABITAT: will thrive on poor soils and most positions but keeps its colour better in sunny positions.

CONDITIONING: split ends and long drink.

Magnolia

M. *stellata*: most varieties of magnolia are too large for a small garden but *Magnolia stellata* is a small compact deciduous shrub. The branches bend and curve bearing small flowers with waxy strap-like petals in early spring. One or two cut and arranged on their own in a tall glass vase or jug are effective.

HABITAT: flowers must be protected from early morning sun, and it should be planted in peat or leafmould.

CONDITIONING: split the ends, proceed with boiling water treatment and long drink.

Philadelphus (mock orange)

One of the most beautiful deciduous flowering shrubs used constantly by flower arrangers. There are many varieties including a good selection of smaller shrubs. The flowers vary from small single to double, white and cream in colour – many are scented. They are ideal for wedding groups and large mixed summer vases. The flowers are better seen if most of the leaves are removed. Among the many good hybrids are:

'Belle-Etoile': decorative single white flowers flushed with maroon.

'Boule d'argent': a good small shrub with white double flowers.

'Manteau-d'Hermine': compact shrub flowering profusely in June. It has small, double, creamy fragrant flowers.

P. *coronarius* 'Aurea': worth growing for the yellow foliage. The tiny cream flowers are disappointing.

HABITAT: any good soil. Likes a sunny position but will also grow in semi-shade.

CONDITIONING: hammer ends, remove most of the leaves and give a long drink, preferably overnight.

Pieris

P. *japonica*: evergreen. New foliage is copper-coloured gradually changing to green. In early spring the branches bear long creamy-white panicles which show well in a tall trumpet vase.

'*Forest Flame*': a new hybrid. The young foliage is bright-red and changes gradually to pink, white and then green. It too has flowers in long drooping panicles.

'*Variegata*': narrow leaves, variegated yellowish-white with young, pink leaves. It is slow growing.

HABITAT: lime-free peaty soil.

CONDITIONING: hammer ends, long drink.

Pittosporum

P. *tenuifolium*: slightly tender evergreen shrub. The stems are covered with pale-green leaves. Small sprays mix well with spring or summer posies. I use it in garlands as it lasts well. There are two varieties that are far more interesting but unfortunately very tender.

'*Garnettii*': a compact shrub with variegated white leaves tinged with pink.

'*Kohutu*': black twigs bearing pale-green undulate leaves. The little dark-brown flowers are inconspicuous in the garden but show up well in a vase.

HABITAT: warm sheltered gardens. '*Kohutu*' flourishes in seaside areas.

CONDITIONING: hammer ends, long drink.

Potentilla

This is a small, deciduous flowering shrub. Arching stems are covered with small star-like flowers from mid-summer until late autumn. There is a good range of different colours, including white, pink, apricot and yellow. I have several varieties and find them extremely useful.

P. *fruticosa*: has many good species including 'Katherine Dykes' which has primrose-yellow saucer-like flowers from May to September.

'*Mandshurica*': creamy-white with small yellow centres.

'*Tangerine*': misty orange.

'*Veitchii*': a small shrub with arching branches and grey leaves and pure-white flowers.

HABITAT: will tolerate some shade but only flowers in full sun.

CONDITIONING: boiling water treatment and long cool drink.

Prunus

In a small garden I would not plant the ordinary Prunus. It takes up too much space and when the flowering season ends it does not provide the flower arranger with interesting foliage. The great exceptions are the autumn flowering varieties – not only are they a joy to behold in the garden but they are the prettiest of flowering shrubs for cutting. There is the white variety P. *Autumnalis*. The stems are covered with tiny star-like flowers with deep-yellowypink stamens. This in fact gives them a faint peachy glow.

P. *subhirtella* '*Autumnalis Rosea*': amazing semi-double shell-pink flowers. The shrubs have graceful bending twigs which make them particularly easy to arrange when cut. I have used the white and pink massed on their own in a well lit church for winter weddings – they make very beautiful groups. A few stems mixed with winter jasmine make a pretty Christmas vase.

HABITAT: if possible site the shrub so that it can be appreciated from a living room window. It is a delight on a winter day. These shrubs need protection from north-east winds which damage early flowers. They flourish in deep moisture retentive soil enriched with a good compost.

CONDITIONING: slit the ends up about two in. and give a long warm drink. If cut well before Christmas in tight bud they will open up gradually.

Pyracantha (firethorn)

This is an evergreen shrub bearing large clusters of orange or yellow berries in the autumn. I like to arrange it in mixed orange and yellow groups with crocosmia, dahlias and bright coloured foliage.

'*Aurea*': yellow berries.

'*Flava*': yellow berries.

'*Lalandei*': orange berries.

HABITAT: any reasonable soil. These shrubs are best trained against a wall or fence in a small garden.

CONDITIONING   hammer ends and long drink. The berries will remain longer if they are sprayed with hairspray.

Pyrus

P. *salicifolia* '*Pendula*' (*weeping pear*): a good tree for a restricted space and makes an attractive focal point in small gardens. It has arching branches reaching to the ground covered with pointed, grey leaves, and in the spring small, white flowers. I like to cut off weeping stems to put in the front of pedestal arrangements. They cascade down and prevent the arrangement from being too stiff.

HABITAT: sunny position, well-drained soil.

CONDITIONING: hammer ends and long drink in warm water. When the stems are in flower give the branches at least 12 hours in water.

Rhododendron

This large family of shrubs includes the evergreen variety and the Azalea. The evergreen shrubs vary in size from medium shrubs to tall trees. In woodland areas and large gardens they are of course superb – huge mop-like flower heads sitting in frills of dark-green leaves, the colours ranging from white through pale-pink to bright-red and the wild R. *ponticum*, which is pale-mauve. They provide ideal material for large groups. As we are concerned in this book with growing flower arranging material for small gardens I would suggest that camellia, which flourishes in the same lime-free soil and woodland areas, is a more suitable flower arranger's shrub. When the flowers are over the foliage is much prettier.

Azaleas are very attractive members of the rhododendron family and more suited to small gardens. They have arching stems bearing either bell-like or tunnel-shaped flowers in many colours. I particularly like the cream, apricot and orange shades – they make a splendid contribution to cream and white groups or clashing reds.

Azalea 'Kaempferi': one of the best azaleas for flower arrangers. It is a semi-evergreen shrub loosely branched. The small clusters of funnel-shaped flowers vary in colour from buff to orange and rosy-scarlet. I like the buff colour arranged with cream and white flowers, and the orange and scarlet varieties look superb in a clashing red group. They flower in May and June.

HABITAT: lime-free soil. The evergreen rhododendron likes semi-shade and woodland areas but the azalea will flourish in sun provided it is in good moisture-retentive soil. It should be watered in dry weather.

CONDITIONING: split the ends very carefully. Give boiling water treatment and, if possible, give them a 12 hour drink in a cool place.

Ribes sanguineum
This is a hardy flowering shrub. In the spring small pink or red tassel-like flowers hang from bare stems as the leaves follow later. I like the flowering stems mixed with the lime-green *Helleborus foetidus* – that combination looks effective against green or white walls.

R.s. 'Pulborough Scarlet': a good deep red variety.

R.s. 'Tydeman's White': a very pale, subtle pink – mixes well with the deeper varieties.

HABITAT: any reasonable soil and prefers sun.

CONDITIONING: hammer ends and give a long drink. When first cut and put into water it does emit a rather nasty smell but this soon disappears.

Rosa (roses)
In the section headed Climbers, I have explained that it is more practical in a small garden to concentrate on these varieties. However, there are exceptions to every rule and the fairy or miniature roses would be one – the 'Queen Elizabeth' would be another and the enchanting small-flowered 'Cecile Brunner'. Also, there are one or two varieties that should be allowed a place simply for their foliage and decorative hips. Some of the 'repeat-flowering' varieties will go on until late November. My Iceberg gave me some perfect unblemished buds at Christmas-time which was a great bonus. The following are just a few of the many roses that cut and last well:

'Cecile Brunner': it will eventually become a large bush carrying a mass of tiny buff-pink small roses presented in sprays. I often use it for brides' headdresses or arrange them massed in little baskets.

'*Pascali*': a white hybrid tea rose that has exceptional large, white flowers like carnations.

'*Queen Elizabeth*': a floribunda with pink flowers opening up from large buds, both of which are splendid in pedestal groups. It will grow up to 12 ft.

Among the small fairy roses which do so well in front of borders or in tubs are:
'*Sweet fairy*': apple blossom pink.
'*Tinkerbell*': red.

There are some roses that have very decorative foliage. They make large shrubs so that there would possibly be space for only one of the following:
R. *nitida*: brilliant autumn foliage and good hips.
R. *rubrifolia*: silvery-purple leaves and bright-orange hips.

If you are near St Albans do visit the Royal National Rose Society. It has delightful gardens laid out to show an enormous variety of roses – sometimes mixed with other climbers and different plants which is very helpful.

HABITAT: well drained soil in sunny position. Regular feeding with rose fertiliser.

CONDITIONING: boiling water treatment plus half a cup of sugar. This should be dissolved in the boiling water – then long drink.

Rosmarinus

R. *officinalis* (*rosemary*): long stems covered in small, evergreen leaves and in spring and summer blue, hooded flowers.

HABITAT: sunny sheltered spot in a well-drained soil.

CONDITIONING: hammer ends and give it a warm drink.

Ruta

R. *graveolens* (*rue*): a very popular shrub with blue-grey glaucous foliage that mixes well with most colours except its own limey-yellow flowers. They are better removed.

'*Variegata*': blue leaflets. Variegated creamy-white foliage.

HABITAT: any well-drained soil and a sunny position.

CONDITIONING: hammer the ends and give long drink in warm water.

Skimmia

S. × '*Foremanii*': a strong-growing female form.

S. *japonioca*: this compact shrub is perfect for small gardens and lasts well. It has little rosettes of dark and sometimes bleached green leaves and scarlet berries at Christmas going on into February and March. To obtain a berried plant there has to be a male and a female shrub. In seaside, warm areas it grows much taller with bleached, almost white, branches and much yellower leaves which make a spectacular shrub for cutting. Large branches mixed with spring flowers and darker foliage make a very good group. When the shrubs are smaller there are still attractive short stems to mix with spring and summer flowers.

S. *japonica* '*Fragrans*': a male plant with dense panicles of white flowers scented like Lily-of-the-Valley.

HABITAT: any reasonable soil in sun or partial shade.

CONDITIONING: hammer ends and long drink. It is a very long lasting shrub. I have had it for at least a fortnight in a coolish room.

Sorbus (mountain ash or rowan)

This orange-berried tree with fern-like leaves is a familiar sight but rather too large for smaller gardens.

S. *vilmorinii*: one of the Chinese species; it is much smaller and counts as a shrub. It has very attractive ferny foliage and large clusters of roseate berries.

HABITAT: any reasonable soil and sun or shade.

CONDITIONING: hammer ends and long drink.

Spiraea

The Spiraea is a large family of deciduous shrubs.

S. *Arguta* '*Bridalwreath*': in April and May, long arching stems are covered in tiny fresh-green leaves and a mass of little white flowers. It is the perfect shrub to cut and use in vases for bridal groups.

S. × *bumalda* '*Anthony Waterer*': worth growing primarily for its vivid foliage – often variegated cream and pink. The flowers are large and flat and deep-carmine in colour. It is a very striking plant both in the garden and cut to mix with other pink and cream flowers. It also has good seed heads.

HABITAT: any good garden soil preferably in a sunny position. They must not be allowed to dry out – 'Anthony Waterer' in particular.

CONDITIONING: for 'Bridalwreath' hammer ends and give long drink. 'Anthony Waterer' needs boiling water treatment.

Symphoricarpus (snowberry)

This is one of my favourite berried shrubs – long, slim, arching sprays bearing snow-white or pink-blushed berries, that are spectacular when arranged on their own against a strong coloured wall or mixed with other flowers. I find a tall jug makes an ideal container (see colour pl. 2). The berries show up if some of the leaves are removed.

S. '*Mother of Pearl*': a delight to pick. The stems bear large clusters of white berries flushed with deep-clover-pink. These autumn fruited shrubs mix well with late summer roses and Michaelmas daisies.

S. '*White Hedger*': an upright growing shrub producing clusters of small white berries.

HABITAT: will grow in most soils but will fruit less well if planted in crowded conditions. In any case the shrub needs to stand out so that the habit of growth is appreciated.

CONDITIONING: hammer stems and give good drink. Remove some of the leaves so that the berries can be seen better.

Syringa (lilac)

Deciduous shrub bearing large flowering panicles in late spring. The colours vary from the palest-mauve to deep-pink and purple. There are also excellent yellow and white varieties which look well in pedestal groups. There are so many good ones it is hard to choose between them.

'*General Pershing*': deep purple-violet heads and late flowering.

'*Madame Lemoine*': large white trusses – an excellent shrub for white and cream groups.

'*Primrose*': pale-primrose-yellow heads, smaller than some varieties.

HABITAT: thrive on any good soil and are happy on lime or chalk. They prefer an open position.

CONDITIONING: hammer the ends and long drink. Remove leaves to ensure the flowers last better and are better seen. The leaves will last in water on their own.

Viburnum

There are several excellent winter flowering viburnums. Their leafless chestnut-coloured branches bear clusters of small flowers, some pink, some white and some scented. I like to mix a few sprays with coloured leaves.

V. × *bodnantense*: upright habit of growth. Large white flowers tinged with carmine pink.

V. × *burkwoodii*: semi-evergreen, an excellent shrub. The white flowers bloom from January to May and they too are scented.

V. *farreri*: more commonly known as '*fragrans*'. Clusters of deep rose-red buds open into white tubular flowers very often before Christmas and are sweetly scented.

V. *opulus* '*Sterile*': is a favourite shrub for those searching for interesting green flowers. The branches bear small balls of tiny green flowers gradually becoming white as they mature. I like to cut them in the green stage and emphasize their shape and colour by stripping off most of the leaves. There is another variety that I prefer, which also has green flowers opening up into white but the flowers are flat-faced exactly like lacecap hydrangeas. The shrub is less upright in character so that there are pretty bending stems to cut and arrange. Another bonus is that there is a mass of scarlet berries in the autumn.

V. *opulus* '*Compactum*': the best for a small garden. It has lacecap flowers but translucent fruits.

V. *tinus laurustinus*: a dense evergreen shrub. The foliage is dark-green and rather dominant in a small garden but provides a continuous supply of cut foliage. I use it quite often as a backing to mixed groups. The shrub flowers continuously from October to April. Clusters of tiny pink buds open up into white flower heads.

V. *tinus* 'Eve Price': a more compact shrub. Pink-tinged flowers are followed by very decorative blue fruits.
HABITAT: any reasonable soil and will tolerate some shade.
CONDITIONING: hammer ends and long drink after removing leaves.

Weigela

The weigela has a good habit of growth – long bending stems covered in small bell-like flowers in vivid red and pink shades and a very good white variety. It flowers at the same time as Philadelphus in late spring and early summer. I cut bunches of both these shrubs and use them together in vases mixed with delphiniums and campanulas. They are particularly suitable for pedestal arrangements. The mixed pink and red varieties are a good mixture to add to a clashing red group. There are several good varieties including:
'*Abel Carriere*': soft rose.
'*Avalanche*': white.
'*Bristol Ruby*': ruby red.
'*Variegata*': pale pink flowers that are rather lost among the variegated leaves, but well worth space because the excellent variegated foliage lasts well into the autumn. They last well in water.
HABITAT: any well-drained soil in a sunny position.
CONDITIONING: hammer ends and give long warm drink.

Climbers

Clematis

Every garden must include at least one clematis – a most versatile climbing plant. It will romp up trunks and scramble up walls and fences, providing different coloured backgrounds for shrubs and plants. Not only are there many different coloured flowers but some have attractive evergreen foliage and some charming small seed heads in the autumn.
C. *cirrosa balearica*: evergreen fern-shaped leaves which turn bronze in winter. One or two leaves tucked into a posy of hellebores is very effective, and the plant produces green flowers, in late winter and early spring.
Among the best lasting varieties for cut flowers are:
'*Barbara Jackman*': mauve flowers from the end of May into June.
'*Henryi*': white flowers in the summer.
'*Lincoln Star*': pale pink flowers tinged with white from the end of May and June.
'*Marie Boisselot*': white flowers from the end of May into June.
'*Perle d'azure*': mauve flowers in the summer.
'*The President*': blue flowers from the end of May into June.

C. *tangutica*: yellow lantern flowers and silvery fluffy seed heads that dry well.
HABITAT: roots must be in cool moist soil. Either cover with flag stones or

ground cover. Flourishes in dry aspect. Clematis should always be planted in a deep hole filled with plenty of good compost at the bottom, which the roots must not touch. A layer of top soil on the compost will protect them.

CONDITIONING: unlike most flowers which like to drink warm water, clematis stems must be plunged into deep cold water and left overnight. When choosing stems for cutting try to choose those that have flowers just opened or three quarters of the way open and remove foliage to reduce transpiration from the leaves.

Cobaea

C. *scandens* (*cups and saucers*): an exceptional climber usually grown as an annual. Trumpet- or cup-shaped flowers in pale green or mauve.

HABITAT: sunny position.

CONDITIONING: no special treatment.

Fatshedera

This is a superb climber. The leaves have the best attributes of both fatsia and hedera.

HABITAT: a warm sheltered position.

CONDITIONING: no special treatment.

Hedera helix (ivy)

These vital evergreen climbers are planted everywhere in my garden – up fences and walls, tumbling out of pots, sprawling up trees, and still there are not enough. I use ivy endlessly in all sorts of ways – cascading down from pedestal vases, the leaves cut off and used in garlands, or the variegated ivies mixed with darker evergreen foliage in green groups. I hope I have made the point that ivy in one form or another is essential.

H. *colchica* 'Dentata': variegated large leaves marbled with creamy-yellow.

H. *helix* 'Buttercup': pretty bright-yellow leaves.

H. *helix* 'Cristata': green wavy-edged leaves.

H. *helix* 'Glacier': green leaves margined white.

H. *helix* 'Goldheart': dark-green leaves with a bright-yellow central splash.

HABITAT: any soil and any situation.

CONDITIONING: no special requirements.

Humulus

Humulus lupulus 'Aureus' (*hop*): the golden-leafed hop is a useful deciduous twiner, winding its way up through bush and hedge, leaving an attractive yellow trail as it goes. Large acid-yellow vine-like leaves are effective used on their own as a good focal point in mixed or yellow groups and the long trails will last in water if well conditioned, and droop in a decorative way over the front of vases.

HABITAT: well-drained soil and sun. Any aspect except north.

CONDITIONING: float the leaves for an hour or so. If the long trails are used, dip the ends in boiling water and give long drink. Spray regularly. The leaves preserve well by the carpet method (see page 100).

Jasminum
J. *nudiflorum*: an essential winter flowering shrub that is better trained as a climber – long bare stems are covered in tiny yellow star-like flowers from November to March. I use it constantly mixed with late autumn and winter flowers. At Christmas it makes a welcome splash of colour among evergreens and variegated holly.
HABITAT: will grow anywhere on good, well-drained soil. It flowers more profusely on a sunny wall or fence.
CONDITIONING: hammer ends and give warm drink.

J. *officinale*: a semi-evergreen, vigorous, twining climber. In summer the plant is covered with clusters of white, star-like flowers which are very strongly scented. I have often used sprays of jasmine mixed with white dianthus and small variegated leaves for table decorations. For one party I added ripe and semi-ripe strawberries – it made an unusual and pretty table centre.
HABITAT: any sunny position and any well-drained soil.
CONDITIONING: hammer ends and give warm drink.

Lathyrus
L. *latifolius* (*everlasting pea*): in a small garden this is a more useful form than ordinary sweet-peas, which need space. It lasts very well in water and makes a great contribution to mixed summer groups. I also use it in candle-cup arrangements. It is available in mauve, pink and white.
HABITAT: rich, well-drained soil and sun.
CONDITIONING: cut ends and give long drink.

Lonicera (honeysuckle)
No climber gives more delight than the honeysuckle. It makes its way up and over fences, walls and any host tree that is in its way. It provides long trailing stems with clusters of small trumpet-like flowers in many colours from white to cream to pink and orange – there are also spectacular red hybrids. Many varieties are scented and they flower from winter right through the summer. I love trailing stems cascading over the front of pedestals and large groups or just a few small groups in little mixed bunches. The smaller trails fit well into candle-cups (see page 106). The ordinary common honeysuckle supplies two of the best varieties:
L. *japonica* '*Aureoreticulata*': worth growing for the foliage alone – semi-evergreen. Its stems are covered in oval, bright-green leaves and netted with yellow veins. It will twine its way over any other shrub or fence making a good splash of colour.

L. *periclymenum* 'Belgica': early Dutch, flowering in May. It has purple-red and yellow flowers.
L. *periclymenum* 'Serotina': late Dutch, flowering from July to September. It has cream-pink flushed flowers that are sweetly scented and is deciduous.

There are many other bright-coloured hybrids which can be found at most garden centres.
HABITAT: L. *periclymenum* needs south or west facing; the other two will grow anywhere. All varieties will grow in any good well-drained soil, with their roots in shade.
CONDITIONING: cut the stems and give long drink.

Rosa (Rose)

Shrub roses need lots of space. Therefore, in a small garden I would concentrate on climbers. Choose varieties that are 'repeat flowering' climbers as they will flower throughout the summer. Others may flower only once or twice. 'Albertine' is a good example. Either go to the Royal National Rose Society in St Albans, where roses can be seen in profusion and are well labelled, or any good nursery, preferably those that are rose specialists. The following are good repeat-flowering climbers and excellent for cutting:
'*Compassion*': pink flushed apricot.
'*Golden Showers*': yellow double.
'*Iceberg*': one of the best white roses with pretty pink flushed double buds.
'*Ophelia*': an old-fashioned long-lasting pink double.
'*Schoolgirl*': apricot double.
'*Zephirine Drouhin*': cerise.
HABITAT: prefer south or south west facing walls and well-broken clay soil. Roses will tolerate other soil provided there is a good base of compost and leafmould.
CONDITIONING: hammer ends and give boiling water treatment, plus half a cup of sugar in the boiling water.

Tropaeolum

T. *majus* (*nasturtium*): an easily-grown good flower for cutting. The climbing varieties provide long trails which add to any tall group. Pick in bud as the flowers will open well in water. In a small garden they make useful climbers. The flowers, which come in every shade from cream through to yellow, pink and orange and brown, look good massed together in copper lustre jugs or bowls (see colour pl.5). Some varieties have variegated leaves. 'Gleam hybrids' have semi-double flowers and are scented.
HABITAT: much better on poor soil, otherwise the plant tends to produce too much foliage. Full sun, semi-shade.
CONDITIONING: the long trails need boiling water treatment. Flowers like a long deep drink.

T. *speciosum*: a spectacular climbing plant. It has small scarlet trumpet-like flowers and bright-green leaves. In the North of England and Scotland it is everywhere, clambering up fences and through and over any available tree or shrub. It sets alight a dark, dreary corner. I like to use it in mixed red flower arrangements or with lime-green and grey foliage.

HABITAT: it does best in northern areas but a friend has it in a next door village in Hertfordshire and it flourishes. It must be dug into a good peaty bed with lots of leafmould and very good drainage.

CONDITIONING: cut the stems and give a long drink.

Vitis (vine)

Vines are worth growing, not only for the fruit but because in the autumn there will be different coloured, large, decorative leaves. I cut the leaves and use them in brightly coloured autumn groups, and find the fruit adds special interest to flowers and foliage. There are several good varieties:

V. *amfelopsis brevipedunculata*: has to be planted against a south wall and often a hot summer produces small round bead-like fruits. As they mature the colour changes from purple to dark blue and finally turquoise speckled, like a bird's egg. The leaves become bright yellow.

V. *vinifera* 'Brandt': the leaves colour well, and the black grapes may be eaten, so take your choice!

V. *vinifera* 'Purpurea': pale leaves growing profusely all through the summer, which gradually become purple by November. The trailing vines are covered in claret-coloured leaves and bunches of black ornamental grapes.

HABITAT: plant against a south wall in very well-prepared soil.

CONDITIONING: if the trails of the vine are used the ends should be given boiling water treatment. The fruits need no special treatment.

Herbaceous

Achillea (yarrow)

Achillea is a hardy herbaceous perennial, flowering in July and August. The yellow flat-headed flowers are sometimes offset by grey, feathery foliage.

A. *filipendulina* 'Coronation Gold': sulphur yellow and grey leaves.

A. *taygetea* 'Moonshine': sulphur yellow with grey leaves.

These two are paler than A. *filipendulina* 'Gold Plate', which is a very rich yellow.

HABITAT: well-drained soil, full sun.

CONDITIONING: no special treatment. They dry well.

Alchemilla

A. *mollis*: hardy herbaceous perennial. This is the perfect flower for arranging, with fluffy lime-green heads and pretty scalloped leaves. Unless the flowers are cut before they seed they will overwhelm next year's plants.

HABITAT: any soil anywhere. If the seedlings are transplanted and some placed in sunny spots and some in deep shade and semi-shade this splendid plant will flower all through the summer to late autumn.

CONDITIONING: boiling water treatment and long drink. The flower heads will dry.

Alstroemeria (Peruvian lily)
This is a herbaceous perennial. Tall stems bear heads of tiny trumpet-like flowers. The A. *ligtu* varieties are the best with many good colours, including salmon-pink, bright-pink, and buff-orange and yellow. They are perfect flowers for clashing red groups and they flower in June.

HABITAT: sunny sheltered position, well-drained soil.

CONDITIONING: cut stems on the slant and give long warm drink.

Amaranthus
Amaranthus caudatus 'Viridis' (*love-lies-bleeding*): this is the green version.

HABITAT: sunny position.

CONDITIONING: hammer ends and remove leaves. Long drink. Preserve by hang-dry method.

Anemone
This is a very attractive spring or autumn flowering perennial. The flowers – some double and some single – are set on tall slim stems. They look very elegant arranged in a glass or white vase with the flowering stems of symphoricarpus. The white berries look particularly good with 'White Queen'.

A. *japonica* 'September Charm': single pink flowers from August to October.

A. *japonica* 'White Queen': large white flowers from August to October.

HABITAT: sunny site, good soil.

CONDITIONING: boiling water treatment and give long drink.

Angelica
Hardy perennial, easily grown from seed. Long stems break into small branches bearing green, flat flowers.

HABITAT: sunny position.

CONDITIONING: boiling water treatment. Preserve the flowers by the hang-dry method.

Antirrhinum (snapdragon)
These grow easily from seed and should be treated as an annual. They come in many different colours and are one of the best garden cut flowers.

Pentstemon-flowered 'Bright Butterflies': the prettiest variety, which live up to their name.

HABITAT: sunny position, well-drained soil.

CONDITIONING: a long drink in very deep water.

Aquilegia (Columbine)

An excellent perennial. The tall stalks branch off into small stems carrying bonnet-shaped flowers in many colours. The lacy fern-like,foliage is pretty arranged on its own.

HABITAT: sun or semi-shade.

CONDITIONING: no special treatment.

Aster (Michaelmas daisy)

Michaelmas daisies are the most useful of this species. They are perennial and flower from mid-summer to late autumn. I find the dwarf varieties rather squat and less interesting. The tall varieties abound in every colour from white to mauve and purple, and various pink shades.

A. *amellus* 'King George': blue.

A. × *frikartii*: blue with a yellow eye.

A. *novae-angliae* 'Elma Potschke': a very bright pink – flowering in the summer. Although I prefer the tall varieties, 'Snowsprite', a dwarf variety, has small white flowers.

HABITAT: sunny position and any soil.

CONDITIONING: hammer ends and give long drink.

Astrantia (masterwort)

This fascinating perennial flowers from mid to late summer. The central stalk branches off into little slim stems each bearing a tiny posy of cream flowers, some tinged with acid-green, some pink. They are pure joy and, once established, increase quickly.

A. *major* 'Shaggy': larger flowers than most, cream-tipped with acid-green.

A. *major* 'Sunningdale' *variegated*: perhaps the best of all as in early spring it throws up variegated leaves which gradually get paler as the flowers appear.

A. *maxima*: larger pink flowers and green underneath.

HABITAT: water-retentive soil, sun or partial shade.

CONDITIONING: the flowers need no special treatment but the variegated leaves should be submerged for several hours and occasionally sprayed.

Brunnera

B. *macrophylla* 'Variegata': hardy herbaceous plant with bright-blue flowers like forget-me-nots, and variegated leaves. It flowers in spring.

HABITAT: semi-shade or shade.

CONDITIONING: boiling water treatment and give long drink.

Calendula (marigold)

This pretty cottage garden flower is a great joy. A hardy perennial in yellow and bright-orange shades, single and double. It lasts well in water and looks splendid massed in a copper lustre container.

HABITAT: sun or semi-shade.

Callistephus

C. *chinensis* (*China aster*): annual single and double daisy-like flower in pink, purple and white. I do not care for the double varieties as they seem to be heavy-headed and dull, but the single variety is charming. I like it arranged in a jug on its own or used with other pink and purple flowers.

HABITAT: sunny position in a loamy soil.

CONDITIONING: split ends and give long warm drink.

Campanula

This is a useful perennial with slender stems bearing cup-like flowers in mauve and white. I use them constantly in summer groups and pedestal vases.

C. *glomerata 'superba'*: violet blue. Flowers from June to July.

C. *latifolia 'Alba'*: long sprays of white flowers from May to June.

C. *persicifolia 'Telham Beauty'* very large handsome blue flowers from June to August.

HABITAT: moist soil and sunny aspect.

CONDITIONING: no special treatment.

Chrysanthemum

This is a very wide group which include shasta daisies, marguerites, and pyrethrum. The shasta daisies are invaluable, some growing to about four ft and the smaller marguerites are a joy to arrange. Spray chrysanthemums are available in shops all the year, so I would concentrate on border varieties which are not.

C. *carinatum 'Tricolour'*: single daisy-like flowers with striking rings of yellow, purple and red, only about two ft in height. They are hardy annuals.

C. *frutescens* (*marguerite*): this shrubby daisy flowers the whole summer. The small white flower with a yellow centre I use constantly arranged in small vases with grey or variegated leaves.

C. *spectabilis*: a pretty annual with white daisy-like flowers with yellow centres.

HABITAT: ordinary garden soil and a sunny position.

CONDITIONING: hammer ends and give long drink.

C. *'shasta daisy'*: these perennial daisies look superb when cut and arranged in large groups and equally pretty in small vases. No garden should be without them. The best varieties for cutting are:

'Mayfield Giant': large creamy white flowers from July to September.

'Silver Princess': single white daisy from June to August.

HABITAT: well-drained soil, sun or partial shade.

CONDITIONING: no special treatment.

Clarkia

This is a hardy annual that flowers in July. It has a good colour range from deep-purple to pink and white and lasts very well in water.

HABITAT: any well-drained soil. It likes sun.

CONDITIONING: boiling water treatment.

Convallaria (lily of the valley)

C. *majalis*: small bell-like flowers hang from pale-green arching stems and are very sweetly scented. They are best massed in a bowl surrounded by their own leaves. They are perennial and increase each year.

HABITAT: dappled shade, moist soils.

CONDITIONING: pick and place in deep water.

Cosmos

C. *bipinnatus*: a useful annual – slender branching plants carrying large flowers in white, pink and purple shades. It lasts very well and its wiry stems make it easy to arrange.

HABITAT: sun and well-drained soil.

CONDITIONING: no special treatment.

Crocosmia

C. *'Lucifer'*: this excellent perennial flowers from June to September. It has brilliant flame-red flowers with sword-like foliage and is a superb addition to red groups. It also has useful pointed tops.

HABITAT: well-drained sunny soil.

CONDITIONING: no special treatment. The leaves dry well with the under carpet method.

Cynara

C. *cardunculus* (*cardoon*): a very useful perennial of the artichoke family – grown primarily for superb blue-grey leaves. Ideal for any large pedestal group. Good seed heads too.

HABITAT: any soil.

CONDITIONING: keep the leaves well sprayed. The seed heads will preserve by hang-dry method.

Delphinium

These tall pointed perennials are superb. Three or five stems arranged in a large group make a great impact. The colours range from white to pale-pink and every shade of mauve and purple. Among the best are:

'Astolat': pink

'Black Knight': purple.

'Galahad': white.

HABITAT: good well manured soil, sunny position. Protect new growth from slugs.

CONDITIONING: the best method is to turn the flowers upside down and fill the hollow stem with water and plug with cotton wool. The alternative is to give them boiling water treatment and a long drink.

Dianthus

D. *barbatus* 'Summer Beauty': a good, annual sweet william. A bushy plant flowering in July and August with all the mixed reds and salmon pink colours associated with this flower.

HABITAT: sun or semi-shade.

CONDITIONING: hammer ends and give long drink. They can be preserved by the hang-dry method.

Dianthus border pinks: no garden can have too many dianthus. These spray carnations are the perfect flower for cutting. They are every colour from white, yellow, pink, scarlet and red, as well as the old-fashioned bi-coloured.

'Doris': peachy pink. A very good cut flower.

'Hayter': a hybrid with white flowers almost as big as carnations. A perfect flower for white groups.

HABITAT: open, sunny position, well-drained soil.

CONDITIONING: no special treatment.

Dicentra

D. *spectabilis* (*bleeding heart*): an unusual perennial flowering in May. The lacy delicate leaves spring from arching stems from which hang tiny heart-shaped flowers, rosy-red with white inner petals. This unusually graceful flower is a sheer joy to arrange and lasts well.

HABITAT: sun or part shade.

CONDITIONING: long drink.

Digitalis (foxglove)

Foxgloves are one of the essential perennials which every flower arranger must grow. They have tall graceful spires that carry white or pink flowers up to a point. There are also yellow and apricot hybrids.

D. *grandiflora*: yellow flowers.

D. *purpurea* 'Excelsior': an excellent strain; white and cream, and pink and mauve flowers.

HABITAT: sun or shade, most soils.

CONDITIONING: a long warm drink.

Doronicum

A useful perennial yellow daisy flowering in April and May. I like to cut a large bunch and arrange them with a few variegated leaves.

HABITAT: sun or part shade.

CONDITIONING: very warm drink.

Echinops (globe thistle)

Tall growing perennial. Large thistle-like heads which dry well by the hang-dry method.

HABITAT: any well-drained soil. It needs a sunny site.

CONDITIONING: hammer the ends and give long drink.

Eremurus (foxtail lily)

This is an exceptional perennial. It has stems covered in starry flowers in many colours and is ideal for summer pedestal arrangements.

HABITAT: sheltered position, sun and well-drained soil.

CONDITIONING: no special treatment.

Erigeron (fleabane)

This plant has arching stems bearing daisy-like flowers. It is a useful perennial flowering from June or August, often later. The colours vary from pink to mauve and purple.

'Azure Fairy': lavender blue flowers from July or August.

'Pink Jewel': pink flowers from July or August.

HABITAT: moist well-drained soil in either sun or part-shade.

CONDITIONING: no special treatment.

Gentiana (gentian)

A beautiful small perennial with bright or deep-blue trumpet-shaped flowers that look excellent arranged in a small bowl with variegated leaves.

G. acaulis: suitable for rockeries. It is spring flowering.

G. asclepiadea: the best for flower arrangers – taller arching stems bear flowers in August.

HABITAT: peaty soil, sun or semi-shade.

CONDITIONING: pick when fully open. Long drink in warm water.

Geranium

G. wallichianum (Buxton's variety): my favourite of all. A hardy perennial which every garden should include. It has delicate, saucer-shaped flowers banded with blue and white centres with purple-black anthers. It flowers from September to November and has enchanting leaves which gradually turn pink and red.

HABITAT: water retentive soil, any position.

CONDITIONING: long warm drink. Remove dead flowers and the buds will continue opening.

Gypsophila

This is one of the prettiest perennials for cutting and is double and single flowered. It looks enchanting in mixed posies or in large bridal groups.

G. paniculata 'Bristol Fairy': tiny, double, white flowers from June to August.

G. *paniculata* '*Snowflake*': double white frothy heads from June to September.
HABITAT: open sunny position and well-drained soil.
CONDITIONING: long deep drink.

Helichrysum (everlasting flower)

This is a half-hardy annual, usually grown for winter dried arrangements. It has daisy-like flower heads in orange, yellow and red.
HABITAT: full sun and poorish well-drained soil.
CONDITIONING: give boiling water treatment and a long drink. Preserve by hang-dry method. They must be picked when fully opened.

Heuchera

H. *sanguinea*: a favourite perennial. From slender stems hang small bell-like flowers, starting green and gradually becoming pink, scarlet and white. It flowers from July to September.
Bressingham Hybrids: pale pink to deep crimson.
'*Scintillation*': bright pink tipped coral.
HABITAT: well-drained soil, partial shade. A mulch or peat in spring makes better flowers.
CONDITIONING: no special treatment.

Hosta

Flower arrangers love hostas – not so much for the flowers which are often rather dull but for the leaves which are beautifully shaped – some tiny and some quite large and important. Some have cream markings and curled edges. They make the perfect focal point in large and small groups.
H. *fortunei albo-marginata*: pretty leaves edged with cream as well as mauve flower spikes. It flowers from July to August.
H. *fortunei* '*Albo picta*': yellow leaves edged green and mauve. It flowers from July.
H. *sieboldiana* '*Elegans*': large blue-green leaves, lilac flowers from June to July. It is particularly suitable for pedestal and large groups.
H. '*Thomas Hogg*': broad leaves edged creamy-white. It also has mauve flowers which, unlike most varieties, are as good as the leaves.
H. *undulata*: very pretty wavy leaves and mauve flowers in July.
HABITAT: semi-shady, moist areas. You must de-slug constantly.
CONDITIONING: float for an hour or so and spray in hot weather.

Iberis (candytuft)

I. *amara*: the best variety with large white flowers. It is a useful annual, flowering from July to September.
HABITAT: sunny border.
CONDITIONING: no special treatment.

Kniphofia (red hot poker)

The poker-like stems rise up from long sword-like leaves and make a useful pointed shape for pedestals and formal groups. They are hardy perennials and flower from June on into autumn. There are many striking colours including:

K. 'July Glow': bright buttercup-yellow.

K. 'Maid of Orleans': a subtle buff colour fading into white.

K. 'Mount Etna': vivid scarlet.

HABITAT: full sun, well-drained soil. In very exposed areas they may need some protection.

CONDITIONING: slice the ends of the stems at an angle and give long drink in warm water.

Lobelia

L. cardinalis: dramatic dark red spikes with small, butterfly, scarlet flowers, offset by deep-red leaves. It is the perfect addition to clashing red groups.

HABITAT: ordinary moist soil. Sun or light shade.

CONDITIONING: long drink after boiling water treatment.

Lunaria (honesty)

Lunaria biennis: hardy biennial grown primarily for winter preservation. Purple flowers in the spring which I find dull, but after a while green seed heads appear which arrange well in green groups. Later the outer part dries. This is removed to reveal a satiny partition which is very useful in winter groups or Christmas decorations.

HABITAT: any soil, any position.

Matthiola (stock)

Stock comes in several varieties and is an excellent cut flower. It has rounded columns, covered in small flowers in many colours from white to mauve, pink and red.

'Brompton': a hardy biennial flowering late spring or early summer.

'East Lothian': hardy biennual flowering early summer.

HABITAT: plant near a window as they are scented in a sunny position.

CONDITIONING: hammer ends and give long warm drink.

Moluccella

M. laevis (bells of Ireland): a very popular annual. Green shell-like flowers grow up the stems. I prefer them preserved in glycerine when they turn parchment colour – invaluable in winter dried arrangements.

HABITAT: well-drained soil, sun.

CONDITIONING: remove all leaves to reveal the flowers.

Myosotis (forget-me-not)

This is a hardy perennial that seeds like mad. It has pretty blue flowers in April and May.

HABITAT: any sunny or semi-shady position.

CONDITIONING: long drink.

Nepeta

A hardy herbaceous perennial, Nepeta has slender spikes of purple flowers in June and July. It makes a useful outline to many small mixed bunches.

HABITAT: sunny position.

CONDITIONING: no special requirements.

Nicotiana

N. *alata* (*tobacco plant*): half hardy annual in soft pale colours as well as a deep wine colour. Most popular of all is 'Limelight' which is green. It has lovely star-like flowers and attractive bendy stems. Strongly scented in the evening.

HABITAT: well-drained soil and sunny position.

CONDITIONING: long drink in warm water.

Nigella (love-in-the-mist)

This is a hardy annual with pale-blue flowers set off by pretty, feathery, green leaves.

HABITAT: sun or semi-shade.

CONDITIONING: the silvery seed-heads are often splashed with pink or mauve. Remove outer leaves and hang-dry.

Paeonia (paeony)

This is a hardy herbaceous shrubby perennial that flowers in late spring or early summer. The herbaceous paeonies have superb rounded heads of flowers varying from white to pale- and deep-pink and red. These are perfect flowers for any large group. The foliage often turns red in the autumn. There are very pretty single varieties. My favourite is:

P. *lactiflora*: white flowers with huge golden stamens.

HABITAT: sunny position or semi-shade. Well-drained soil.

CONDITIONING: slice ends and give long warm drink.

Papaver (poppy)

I love all poppies. Unfortunately, the large oriental poppy takes up too much space in a small garden and so I would concentrate on the smaller varieties.

P. *nudicaule*: has pretty single flowers in salmon-pink and orange, which are lovely arranged with grey foliage.

P. *rhoeas*: the Shirley poppy. It is an excellent annual with the same colour range. They flower all summer.

HABITAT: sun and semi-shade.

CONDITIONING: boiling water treatment. Keep the seed heads for drying.

Passiflora (passion flower)

P. *caerulea*: the passion flower has a very exotic appearance. Pale-creamy-grey flowers with deeply-marked blue centres and handsome evergreen foliage. One or two of the flowers picked and used among purple and green grapes and lime green Nicotiana 'Limelight' make an interesting table decoration for a dinner party. Alternatively, long trailing stems look attractive spilling over a trumpet-shaped vase.

HABITAT: south or west aspect. Needs sun and a sheltered position and well-drained soil.

CONDITIONING: if a trail is used it must have boiling water treatment. The flowers on their own simply require a long drink.

Pentstemon

These plants are one of the prettiest The flowers are like little foxgloves on slender bending stems. They are slightly tender.

'Evelyn': a smaller plant with pale-pink flowers.

'Garnet': pretty deep-red flowers.

'Sour Grapes': mauve-tipped pink flowers.

HABITAT: sun and well-drained soil.

CONDITIONING: give boiling water treatment and a long drink.

Phlox

These half-hardy annuals and perennials are very good for cutting. The stems bear large clusters of small flowers in different colours including white and deep-pink and there is also a superb mauve variety – 'Hampton Court'.

HABITAT: sun and semi-shade in most soils. It needs a sheltered site.

CONDITIONING: no special treatment.

Physalis

P. *alkekengi franchetii*(*Chinese lantern*): orange lanterns appear on long trailing stems in August. They should be picked when fully ripe and dried by the hang-dry method for winter groups.

HABITAT: sunny position and well-drained soil.

Polygonatum multiflorum (Solomon's seal)

The most superb perennial. The arched stems bear long wands of dark-green pointed leaves and tiny cream bell-like flowers hanging beneath. It is perfect for large groups.

HABITAT: shady area in a leafy, moisture-retentive soil.

CONDITIONING: no special treatment.

Primula

This large family includes primulas, polyanthus, primroses and auricula, all of them invaluable spring-flowering perennials. Polyanthus come in a huge range of colours. I like them arranged in a bowl surrounded by their own leaves. Apart from the wild primrose there are many coloured ones, some single, some double.

P. *auricula*: the most beautiful of all. The many-clustered head bears flowers in brilliant colours, each one looking hand-painted – buff, purple, cream, red and yellow. Very pretty pale fleshy-green leaves.

HABITAT: will tolerate full sun but must have water-retentive soil.

CONDITIONING: long drink and deep water.

P. × *'Garryarde'*: an interesting variety. It has effective dark-bronze leaves which set off the pale-coloured flowers to perfection.

HABITAT: leafy peaty moist soil, dappled shade.

CONDITIONING: Polyanthus should have boiling water treatment. Primroses need no special conditioning.

Pulsatilla

P. *vulgaris* (*pasque flower*): a small hardy perennial with delightful lavender-purple, bell-like flowers in April and May, followed by silver seed heads.

HABITAT: sunny site, well-drained soil.

CONDITIONING: boiling water treatment. The seed heads dry well by the hang-dry method.

Pyrethrum

P. *roseum*: perennial with double and single daisies. Colours vary from pink, crimson, scarlet and white, all flowering in the summer.

HABITAT: sunny position and well-drained soil.

CONDITIONING: Needs no special treatment.

Rudbeckia

R. *hirta* (*black-eyed Susan*): a perennial that is a great favourite. The stems branch off to yellow daisy-like flowers with hard, almost black, cone-like centres which dry well when the petals fall. There are good dwarf varieties which come in many shades of yellow and brown flowering from mid-summer into autumn.

HABITAT: sunny position and good soil.

CONDITIONING: no special treatment. Preserve seed heads (see pages 97-9).

Salvia

S. *horminum*: an annual easily grown from seed. The bracts are in many colours, white through pink to purple, flowering all summer.

HABITAT: any soil anywhere.

CONDITIONING: no special treatment.

Saxifraga

S. *umbrosa* (*London Pride*): a dainty pink perennial which flowers from May to June.

HABITAT: sun or shady position.

CONDITIONING: no special treatment.

Scabiosa

S. *caucasica*: annual and perennial. Beloved by flower arrangers, these flat-faced flowers are immensely decorative. The green frilled buds are often used separately in tiny vases. The flowers vary from white to pale and deep mauve and blue.

'*Bressingham White*': almost a green flower. The centres are filled with tiny green buds surrounded by whitish-green petals.

'*Clive Greaves*': blue flowers from summer into early autumn.

HABITAT: dislikes clay, requiring well-drained soil in sunny position.

CONDITIONING: if possible give long drink over night.

Sedum (ice plant)

This is an excellent hardy perennial. The rounded stems have grey, succulent leaves and in late summer large, flat flower heads, some dusky-pink, some deep red.

S. *spectabile*: large dusky-pink flower heads.

'*Autumn Joy*': a good hybrid, darker and richer in colour.

HABITAT: sun or semi-shade and well-drained soil.

CONDITIONING: no special treatment. The flower heads dry well by the hang-dry method.

Sisyrinchium

This is a hardy perennial. In June pale-yellow flowers; later, it has excellent seed heads which turn mahogany-brown.

HABITAT: any soil in sun or semi-shade.

CONDITIONING: boiling water treatment. The seed heads hang-dry well.

Solidago

S. '*goldenmosa*' (*golden rod*): a perennial. This is much the best variety. Tall stems bear bright golden-yellow spires from late summer through autumn.

HABITAT: sun and well-drained soil, will tolerate chalk and clay.

CONDITIONING: no special treatment. Will dry by the hang-dry method.

Thalictrum (meadow rue)

This is a useful perennial. Tall stems bear fluffy yellow and purple flowers. The finely-cut feathery foliage lasts well in water.

HABITAT: sun and well-drained soil.

CONDITIONING: the foliage should float for several hours in a bath.

Verbascum

These flowery spikes are useful in pedestal and large groups. They are a biennial and perennial herb with pink and yellow flowers in the summer. When the petals fall there are large useful seed heads.

V. *bombyciferum*: probably the best variety. A biennial with silver foliage and spikes of pale-yellow flowers in the summer.

HABITAT: at the back of any sunny border on dry light soil, also thrives on chalk.

CONDITIONING: hammer ends, long drink. It can be preserved by the hang-dry method.

Viola (pansy, violet)

Pansies have large faces with clearly defined markings. Now that there are good winter flowering varieties, they flower throughout the year. Sutton's 'giant pansy' is a very good strain and invaluable for small vases.

HABITAT: sun or shade – a good edging plant.

Violettas: miniature tufted violas which look enchanting in tiny vases.

HABITAT: rock gardens or edges.

CONDITIONING: no special treatment.

Zinnia

This is a half-hardy annual flowering in late summer and early autumn. It has large flat daisy-like flowers in vivid colours. The green Zinnia 'Envy' is the best.

HABITAT: rich soil, full sun.

CONDITIONING: long drink. It is advisable to put a stub wire up the stem to prevent it bending.

Bulbs, corms, tubers and rhizomes

I wonder whether there are readers who are as confused as I used to be over the difference between bulbs, corms, tubers and rhizomes? All serve as a means of food storage; this is necessary when the plant is dormant. Together they can be described as bulbous plants, but individually they have their own special characteristics.

A **bulb** is a thick underground bud with fleshy scales, the roots of which die annually. Tulips and daffodils are typical. A **corm** is a modified stem and unlike the bulb it has no scales. Cyclamen is an example. A **tuber** is a fleshy underground stem containing buds. In the case of a dahlia they appear on the top, while a potato has buds all over the tuber. A **rhizome** is a prostrate stem running horizontally, partly underground, bearing both roots and shoot buds. Iris is a typical example.

The difference is important because bulbs, corms and rhizomes can be left undisturbed, and so can be planted under shrubs and among herbaceous plants. On the other hand tubers such as dahlias cannot in unsheltered districts be left safely in the ground during the winter.

In our garden all the small narcissi, scillas, muscari and snowdrops are never moved. Unfortunately , however, the taller varieties of daffodils and also tulips have sometimes to be lifted to make space for other plants; otherwise they would also be left undisturbed. Bulbs must, however, be left in the ground for six weeks after they have stopped flowering. The leaves will feed the bulbs. It is quite unnecessary to tie the leaves into the ugly little bunches which one sometimes sees: in fact to tie them stops much of the goodness returning to the bulbs. It is desirable when the flowers fade to give the bulbs a feed of any general fertiliser. This will ensure that they receive added nourishment and will undoubtedly encourage more growth and much larger flowers the following year. After six weeks the foliage can be cut down and if the bulbs have to be lifted they can be stored in a dry place.

We used to have a mass of bulbs in grass underneath a tree, but we found that this was not a good idea in a small garden. It was a wonderful sight for a few weeks when the crocus and daffodils were in full bloom, but for the rest of the year we were left with untidy uncut grass. Instead we now have pretty ground cover plants underplanted with bulbs and corms, with cyclamen and colchicum added for autumn flowering.

It surprises me that so many people still think of bulbs only in terms of daffodils and tulips, forgetting that bulbous plants provide a huge range of fascinating flowers throughout the year, from the tiniest snowdrop to the tallest lily. In the summer when you are lying in the garden look about you and see where bulbs might best be planted. Send for catalogues from specialist nurseries. They may prove to be more expensive, but they undoubtedly offer the best range of unusual and interesting varieties. In fact many nurseries list them as specially suitable for floral arrangements. I have sometimes been tempted in local markets to buy 'special offers', in other words a bag of mixed bulbs. Very often they have been quite satisfactory, but at other times there has been a proportion of mere dehydrated, rotten little nonentities. If you are buying over the counter, check that the bulbs are firm and of a good size. The better the bulbs are, the better the flowers will be.

Bulbs should be planted deeply: otherwise they will be attacked by frost and they will also suffer from lack of food and water.

There are very many bulbous plants, but I have found that the following will provide a wide range of cut flowers and can be included in a small garden.

Agapanthus (African lily)
Headbourne hybrids: spherical clusters of deep and pale blue flowers from July to September. These blue lilies are a marvellous sight in the garden and cut and last well. I love them mixed with apricot or white flowers.
HABITAT: sheltered site. Must be kept moist in growing season and well-drained in the winter.
CONDITIONING: cut the stems on the slant and long drink.

Allium (ornamental onion)

I have only recently come to appreciate how effective alliums are in a border – they stand up on large stems bearing round ball-like heads comprised of clusters of tiny star-like flowers in different shades, some white, some pink, some mauve. Many of them have superb seed heads that dry well.

A. *christophii*: huge rounded heads of glistening mauvey-pink flowers that dry brown. Summer flowering.

HABITAT: sun.

A. *giganteum*: lilac-purple flower heads on top of very straight tall stems. Excellent when arranged in tall pedestal arrangements.

HABITAT: sun or gentle shade.

A. *karataviense*: medium-height stems bearing spherical silvery-white flower heads, and blue-grey leaves. Spring flowering.

HABITAT: sun and good drainage.

CONDITIONING: put in cold water – hot water brings out the onion smell. The heads dry well with the hang-dry method.

Anemone

The most popular varieties, because they cut and last well, are A. *coronaria*. They are brightly-coloured flowers, single or double mauve, pink, scarlet or white with attractive parsley-like leaves.

A. *blanda*: in spring, these unique starry flowers quite soon form a carpet. The flowers vary from white to pink and mauve. To my great joy I have found that these favourite flowers will last in water.

HABITAT: will quickly form colonies on any reasonable soil.

A. *coronaria* 'De Caen': semi-double.

A. *coronaria* 'St Brigid': single.

HABITAT: well-drained soil, sunny position, and good garden compost.

CONDITIONING: for all anemones boiling water treatment and long drink.

Chionodoxa (glory of the snow)

C. *luciliae*: this little bulb supports tiny arching stems of blue and white star-like flowers. They last well in water and massed together, or, used with other small flowers and leaves, make very pretty spring posies.

HABITAT: any reasonable soil in sun or shade. It is excellent in rock gardens.

CONDITIONING: no special treatment.

Colchicum

Colchicum and autumn crocus are often wrongly named. The crocus has three stamens and the colchicum six. The flowers appear first and then the enormous leaves. Some of these cut well and are useful foliage as they last well in water. Leave some behind on the ground otherwise all goodness will be removed. There are many varieties ranging from white to palest-pink to deep-mauve. I have them planted in among ajuga – the dark leaves show up the flower to perfection.

'*Album*': large white goblet-like flower.

'*The Giant*': one of the biggest, mauvish-pink with white base.

'*Waterlily*': pinky mauve.

HABITAT: rich leafy soil under trees and shrubs.

CONDITIONING: arrange in fairly deep water.

Crocus

There are many varieties flowering from late winter into spring. The yellow seem to be more popular with the birds. Among the good Dutch types is C. *aureus*, which is yellow and flowers in early spring. My personal favourite is C. *tomasinianus* flowering mid-winter to early spring. The slender buds open up into star-like flowers, mauvish-blue on the outside and bright cream-mauve inside. They are very hardy and increase each year.

HABITAT: any ordinary well-drained soil. Crocus will do well under trees.

CONDITIONING: place the flowers in water up to the base of the flower and arrange with its tall spiky leaves.

Cyclamen

This is an enchanting little reflexed-petalled flower appearing in late summer, autumn and spring, followed by heart-shaped leaves – deep green with paler markings. I use the leaves constantly with mixed posies and love the flowers massed together.

C. *coum*: flower in mid-winter to spring. Quite hardy pink- and white-flowered varieties with plain or marbled ivy-shaped leaves.

C. *neopolitanum*: flowers in the autumn – white or pink flowers. It has well-marked leaves which appear after the flower.

HABITAT: dappled shade, under trees or shrubs. It needs peaty leafy soil that does not dry out.

CONDITIONING: no special treatment.

Dahlia

A half-hardy tuber rooted perennial with a very wide colour range. The flowers vary from small pom-pom to large decorative blooms. Some have attractive bronze or dark foliage and they flower from July to the first frost. They are very useful in all mixed autumn groups. The decorative variety have large double blooms and include the water-lily – this has less petals and in fact resembles its name-sake and is, I think, the prettier of the two. These large flowers are very effective in pedestal groups. The cactus dahlia is also double but with pretty pointed and narrower petals. The collerette or anemone is unusual – it has single flowers with a 'collar' of tiny flowers forming a central disc. The little pom-pom dahlia is quite different with small globular heads covered in tiny petals turning inwards. These are dwarf plants which look well in the front of sunny borders. They will not exceed 24 in. in height. We are fortunate in living near to Aylett's Nurseries where we can see every type of dahlia growing. The following are excellent for small gardens and for cutting:

'Autumn Lustre': reddish-orange, small decorative water-lily.

'Dazzler': miniature decorative only about I ft in height with scarlet flowers and dark foliage.

'Easter Sunday': attractive creamy-white collerette.

'Winter Dawn': pale yellow water-lily with a lilac tinge.

'Yellow Hammer': dwarf plant with pretty yellow single flowers and attractive foliage.

HABITAT: moist, well-drained soils. Dahlias must not be planted before the danger of frost is passed. The tubers should be planted in peat. When the first frost arrives they must be lifted; the peat will then fall away leaving a clean tuber. They should be dried and stood upside down to allow all moisture to drain away. Treat with Benlate and store in wooden boxes packed with peat or sand in a frost-free place.

CONDITIONING: boiling water treatment and long drink.

Endymion

E. hispanicus (Spanish bluebell): much as I love the common bluebell, this is a better variety. The flowers are large so show up better in the border and are more useful for flower arranging.

E.h. 'Excelsior': deep-blue.

E.h. 'Mount Everest': white.

E.h. 'Queen of the Pinks': rose-pink.

HABITAT: forms large clumps. Spanish bluebells are better in woodland or shady borders.

CONDITIONING: both for cultivated varieties and the wild bluebell cut stems fairly short and give long drink in warm water.

Erythronium

The grey-green spotted leaves in themselves are worth growing but added to that are the pink, white and yellow pagoda-like flowers, appearing in spring.

E. tuolumnense: a taller variety with glossy green leaves and yellow flowers.

HABITAT: dappled shade under trees. A good leafy peaty soil.

CONDITIONING: the flowers last well in water but are fragile so need careful handling. They need a good long drink before arranging. Their own leaves are the perfect background – they should be floated first.

Fritillaria

There are the large crown imperials with orange and yellow flowers hanging from a tuft at the spine and the smaller F. meleagris with tiny chequered bells of purple-pink on creamy white. The Imperial is a good lasting flower and stands well in large groups. The little meleagris is best arranged on its own in a tall wine glass which will reveal the colouring and delicacy to perfection.

F. *imperialis*: place the bulbs deep and on their side in moisture-retentive soil in full sun.

F. *meleagris*: plant the bulbs the right way up in moisture-retentive soil in dappled shade.

CONDITIONING: give usual long drink before arranging.

Galanthus (snowdrop)

G. *elwesii*: a giant snowdrop. The white flowers have broad green markings. The leaves are broad and glaucous. This is the perfect variety to arrange on its own with natural foliage in a slender glass vase.

G. *nivalis*: the common snowdrop is one of my favourite spring flowers. Little white bell-like flowers hang from a pale-green slender stem. The double varieties resemble white ballet skirts tinged in the middle with green. I like to mass the flowers together in a low silver bowl either with their own leaves or a frill of tiny ivies.

HABITAT: sun or semi-shade, any soil.

CONDITIONING: usual long drink before arranging. I keep *nivalis* in deeper water than *elwesii*.

Gladiolus

Gladiolus is not my favourite flower. If they can be planted in a space allocated for cut flowers, fine – otherwise they stand like sentinels, bending neither left nor right and make no contribution to the general design. I realize that in large pedestal groups they stand out well but there are other flowers which are far more attractive. The butterfly varieties and the small nanus ones are far prettier – sadly the nanus are only for very warm gardens. Among the butterfly varieties:

'*Green Woodpecker*': reigns supreme as its name indicates and is superb in any green group.

'*Page Polka*': another good one – pale primrose.

The small nanus varieties include 'The Bride', white flowers which go on opening when cut and last very well and there are two good pink varieties: 'Peach-blossom' shell pink and 'Robinette' cerise-pink marked white on lower petals.

HABITAT: Nanus varieties are very tender and so they must have a very sheltered spot and if necessary be protected in the winter by a covering of ashes. The other varieties will flourish in any sunny situation.

CONDITIONING: pick when some lower flowers are showing; they will then continue to open up and last for some time, provided the lower flowers are nipped off as they die.

Hyacinthus (hyacinth)

The ordinary hyacinth is not easy to arrange in any kind of vase. The stems are too thick and stiff – the other snag is that if cut for indoors a nasty hole is left in the border or tub. H. *cynthella* is a much easier flower with taller slender stems bearing small bell-like flowers that look pretty in the garden and cut and arrange well.

H. *cynthella* '*The Bride*': an attractive white colour.

H. *cynthella* '*Princess Victoria*': shell-pink. Both of these look very attractive arranged in baskets or in white china.

HABITAT: any sunny border.

CONDITIONING: long warm drink.

Iris

I find the Dutch Iris boring. It has straight stems with blue and yellow flowers that add little to the garden and not much to flower arrangements. Far more interesting is the bearded iris which has tall stems bearing large, mauve, purple and cream and brown flowers, very clearly veined. I use them often in pedestal groups. Many iris have inconspicuous flowers but useful variegated foliage. However, the ones I like best are the dwarf varieties, I. *reticulata* and I. *unguicularis* for instance. These small treasures nestle happily among other flowers and are the greatest joy to pick. I like to add a few leaves and arrange them in special containers, like wine glasses, small china baskets or jugs.

I. *foetidissima* '*Variegata*': foliage variegated throughout the year.

HABITAT: shade or semi-shade.

I. *reticulata*: deep-blue or violet flowers on short stems flowering in January, February or March.

I. *reticulata* '*Harmony*': deep-blue.

HABITAT: rock gardens in full sun.

I. *unguicularis*: for many years known as *stylosa*. Pale-mauve with gold and white markings. Flowers in winter and early spring. Pick in bud and it will gradually open with a scent of primroses.

HABITAT: as warm a site as possible, preferably against a south wall.

CONDITIONING: no special requirements.

Lilium (lily)

This is too large a subject to dwell upon in any detail. Good specialist nurseries will sell catalogues that not only list every type of lily but will give growing instructions for each variety. Suffice it to say that the lily is the perfect flower for cutting – large pedestal groups are a perfect setting for all lilies. I also love a few stems arranged in a tall elegant vase or jug. Madonna lilies and L. *auratum* look particularly good on their own or in huge summer groups. The new 'Enchantment' lily is useful – unfortunately they have no scent; they come in a vivid red-orange or there is 'Mont Blanc' which is white. I have listed some favourites but there are many more.

L. *auratum*: heavily scented, wide open flowers, cream but clearly marked with reddish-brown. It is one of the most beautiful.

L. *candidum* (*madonna lily*): white flower, golden streamers.
L. *martagon* (*Turk's cap*): tall stems with flowers that are turned back, and a wide range of colours from white, bronze, mauve and even black.
HABITAT: most varieties require sun or partial shade, good leafmould and very well-drained soil. They also flourish in pots or tubs.
CONDITIONING: cut stems at an angle and give long warm drink.

Muscari (grape hyacinth)
I love these easily grown spring bulbs. Short stout stalks bear spikes of white or blue flowers. The white are useful mixed among pale colours but I prefer the blue. Grown in clumps among other small flowers like Polyanthus and dwarf narcissus they make a very vivid contrast in the border and massed together in bowls for the house with tiny variegated ivy leaves, their spiky stems also give interest to a more formally arranged vase.
HABITAT: any bed or border – also window boxes and tubs.
CONDITIONING: no special treatment.

Narcissus, daffodil
I do not have space here to describe narcissi or daffodils – they are all under the narcissi family but daffodils have trumpets. I prefer all the dwarf varieties. They can remain undisturbed in front of the border. Mine are mixed with other spring flowers like muscari and polyanthus, and the type and colour could not be more varied, from white to pale cream and deepest yellow. They mix well with all the other small spring flowers and leaves. The larger varieties may have to be taken up and stored in a dry place when they have finished flowering. It may be helpful to know the different groups that the species come under:

1	*Trumpet* or *Corona*	
2	*Large cupped*	} one flower on a stem
3	*Small cupped*	
4	*Double*	
5	*Triandrus*: one to six flowers per stem	
6	*Cyclamineus*: petals turn upwards like Cyclamen	
7	*Jonquilla*: several to stem and scented	
8	*Tazetta*: bunch flowered	
9	*Poeticus*: white petals, red or red-rimmed flat cups	
10	*Species*: wilder hybrids	
11	*Misc.*:any other	

I do suggest that you send for a bulb catalogue to see the huge choice that is available. The following are some that I enjoy among the dwarf varieties:
N. *bulbocodium* (*the hooped petticoat*): quite distinct large funnel-shaped corona with reduced segments (petals). It resembles a hooped petticoat caught up in the wind. It flowers in mid-spring.
HABITAT: moist areas.

N. *cyclamineus*: these pretty flowers appear before the hooped petticoats and are like cyclamen flowers. They have long tubular coronas with petals reflexed upwards.

HABITAT: prefer moist conditions.

N. *tazetta* 'Geranium': a lovely flower for cutting. It is white with an orange-red corona.

N. *tazetta* 'Ice Follies': a good white flowered narcissus used commercially because it travels and last well.

N. *tazetta*: very pretty pale yellow bunched heads that look good among other spring flowers. They last very well.

N. *triandus albus* (angel's tears): one of the prettiest of the dwarf daffodils. Pendulous, creamy-white flowers with reflexed petals.

Many people love 'King Alfred' but to me they are nasty stiff yellow daffodils that are impossible to arrange in any vase. A much prettier yellow daffodil in my view is the old cottage garden variety 'Van Sion'.

HABITAT: I have given the habitat for the dwarf varieties. The rest will flourish in most places in a well-drained soil. Feed after they have finished flowering.

CONDITIONING: narcissi last better in shallow water.

Nerine

N. *bowdenii* (Guernsey lily): one of my favourite flowers. The bulbs like sitting fairly near the surface and close together and throw up tall thickish stems, topped by a branched head of deep-pink trumpet-like flowers. They flower for several weeks outside, but equally well if cut and used with other flowers and they are the perfect focal point for large groups. I also love to arrange them with grey foliage, and late flowering white roses – 'Iceberg' makes a perfect companion.

HABITAT: full sun, warm border. They hate being moved. If they are split up they will take some time before flowering profusely.

CONDITIONING: cut stems at an angle and give long warm drink.

Schizostylis

S. *coccinea* (kaffir lily): an autumn flowering bulb which makes it very popular. Slender stems bear small star-like flowers reaching up to a point. The leaves are like a narrow iris leaf. The bulbs are expensive but worth every penny. The colours range from a vivid scarlet to crimson and pale pink.

'Major': scarlet-red.

'Mrs Hegarty': rose-pink.

'Vicountess Byng': shell-pink.

HABITAT: warm sunny position. The soil must not be allowed to dry out.

CONDITIONING: no special treatment.

Scilla

S. *bifolia*: small bulbs bearing tiny blue star-like flowers on slender stems. Strap-shaped leaves emerge as the flower opens.

HABITAT: sunny position or semi-shade.

CONDITIONING: give long drink in cold water.

Tulipa (tulip)

I find tulips quite difficult to place in a small garden. The taller varieties like the Darwins have to be removed after flowering to make space for other plants. I much prefer the lily flowering ones. Their graceful pointed petals and slender stems cut well for every sort of container. I use them often in a white cornucopia vase or in large spring groups. The small double varieties that remain undisturbed in the front of the border are also very useful – they cut and last well. There are so many to choose from that I suggest sending for an illustrated catalogue to enable you to make your own choice. The following are old tried favourites and the varieties:

'Artist': an unusual warm apricot and green flower.

T. tarda: a yellow and white dwarf tulip that grows well and can remain undisturbed.

T. greigii: attractive leaves edged with maroon.

T. kaufmanniana: attractive leaves edged with maroon.

T. 'Viridiflora Praecox': of special interest. Creamy-yellow inside and green outside.

'White Triumphator': excellent white lily flowering.

HABITAT: most tulips prefer sun.

CONDITIONING: long warm drink with half a cup of sugar. If the stems wilt then take them out, recut and give a long drink.

Zantedeschia

Zantedeschia aethiopica 'Crowborough' (arum lily): arum lilies and their marvellous large arrow-shaped leaves are a superb addition to white groups or picked and arranged with one or two of their own leaves in a white vase. The creamy waxy-white flower has a yellow central finger (spadix). This new variety is hardy but should be protected in very cold areas.

HABITAT: sunny sheltered position.

CONDITIONING: cut stems on the slant and long drink up to their necks. The leaves should be floated for several hours.

Ground cover

The term ground cover is used to describe plants grown so close together that they form a canopy of leaves which excludes light and air, with the result that weeds cannot survive. In a small garden where every nook and cranny is needed for shrubs and plants there is not much call for this method of planting, but there may be some areas – on banks and under trees, for example – where nothing much besides ground cover will thrive. I have listed those of the smaller species which I have found most useful. Many will do well whether in shade or sun, but I have thought it helpful to draw attention to some of those which will flourish in full shade.

Ajuga

A. *reptans* (*bugle*): these splendid low-growing plants make decorative ground cover. Small oval leaves, some red, some cream and red, and some deep purple bearing a brush-like flower in May, which mixes well when cut with other small flowers. The leaves can be used on their own in miniature posies.

A.R. '*Burgundy Glow*': purple leaves tinged pink.

A.R. '*Multicolor*': the most interesting variety. It has dark purple leaves splashed with cream and pink.

A.R. '*Variegata*': pale grey-green leaf with off white markings.

HABITAT: shade and semi-shade or full sun. 'Variegata' is the only variety which has to be in a sunny position.

CONDITIONING: no special treatment.

Astilbe

A. *chinensis pumila*: the matt green leaves soon make a carpet. Stiff stems thrust up through the leaves bearing clusters of rose-pink flowers. If they are left they will dry naturally providing buff-coloured spikes for dried arrangements.

HABITAT: damp, shady bed.

CONDITIONING: no special treatment.

Campanula

C. *poscharskyana*: a very pretty low-growing ground cover. Small lilac-blue, star-like flowers that mix well with other small flowers.

HABITAT: sunny position and any soil.

CONDITIONING: no special treatment.

Gaultheria

G. *procumbens*: a dwarf shrub that makes good ground cover. The leaves vary from bright-green to pink and red followed by crimson berries.

HABITAT: acid soil semi-shade.

CONDITIONING: soak leaves for about an hour.

Geranium

G. *endressii*: useful variety that will eventually need to be controlled as it seeds itself everywhere. The pretty, pale-pink flowers bloom all summer and will last if conditioned.

HABITAT: sun or shade.

CONDITIONING: give boiling water treatment and a long drink. Dead head the flowers and the buds will continue to open in water.

Lamium

L. *maculatum*: these plants will take over the garden unless controlled. The leaves are variegated and the flowers pale-pink, white or mauve.

L.*m.* '*White Nancy*': silvery leaves, white flowers.

HABITAT: anywhere and everywhere, shade or sun.

CONDITIONING: give boiling water treatment and a long drink.

Polygonum

P. *affine*: flowers from July to October. The spiky stems are covered in tiny shrimp-pink flowers and deeper pink and brown leaves in the autumn.

HABITAT: will grow anywhere but I use it as a ground cover in semi-shade.

CONDITIONING: no special treatment.

Vinca

V. *minor* '*Alba*': this tiny periwinkle has small pointed variegated leaves and little white flowers – a very desirable plant.

HABITAT: shade and any good well-drained soil.

CONDITIONING: boiling water treatment and long drink.

Viola

V. *cornuta*: I count this as a ground cover because it spreads, making a small carpet of tiny purple or white butterfly flowers in June. I arrange them with their own leaves in a small silver bowl.

HABITAT: semi-shade in well-drained soil.

CONDITIONING: arrange in fairly deep water.

Shade and semi-shade loving plants

The following are just a very few of the plants that come into this category:

Bergenia

These evergreen plants are most useful because of their foliage, with rounded leaves often turning red in the autumn.

B. *cordifolia* '*purpurea*': rounded leaves which turn pinky-red at the first sign of frost.

B. '*Baby Doll*': much prettier with pale-pink flowers.

HABITAT: shade or sun, any soil.

CONDITIONING: leaves should be regularly sprayed. Otherwise no special treatment.

Hedera

This has been covered in detail on p. 27 but there are one or two small ivies that do well in shade including 'Green Nipper' and 'Goldheart' and many others with variegated leaves.

HABITAT: shade or semi-shade.

CONDITIONING: no special treatment.

Helleborus

There are many different hellebores, some small, some fairly tall and all beautiful but all are hardy perennials. It is very hard to know which to choose. The obvious first choice for flower arrangers are the green varieties – foetidus particularly looks well in a green group and a great addition to pedestal arrangements. The other hellebores vary enormously, some flowers are pale cream, some maroon, some pure white and they often have contrasting markings – how can one choose? The following list may be helpful:

H. *argutifolius*: flowers early, sometimes in January. It has pretty green cup-like flowers and large coarse spiny-edged leaves like leather fingers.

H. *foetidus*: tall stems with green flowers and dark green hand-like leaves which make useful evergreen foliage. It is spring flowering.

H. *niger*: known more often as the Christmas rose but in fact usually flowers in January and February. Has large creamy-white saucer-like flowers.

H. *orientalis*: perhaps the most beautiful of all. It flowers from February to April. The main stem branches off to side stems bearing flowers in different colours – some cream tinged with green and brown speckled throats, some purple and some burgundy. When the flowers finish they are followed by handsome evergreen leaves. I think this particular variety is better arranged in a vase on its own so that the detail is truly appreciated.

HABITAT: gentle shade or semi-shade and moisture-retentive soil that is well-drained.

CONDITIONING: H. *foetidus* and H. *corsicus* need boiling water treatment and long drink. The other hellebores should be pricked at intervals up the stem to the flower head. The green hellebores last well in water provided they are well conditioned but the others will last only if they are arranged in deep water. If they should wilt take them out, cut the stems and put them in water up to the flower head for about two hours.

Hosta

H. *undulata*: low-growing plant with pointed twisted leaves and wide cream border.

HABITAT: shade and deep rich soil.

CONDITIONING: float the leaves for an hour or so before arranging.

Iris

I. *foetidissima*: an evergreen iris that has long, arching, rich-green leaves. The flower is pale yellow marked with dark-brown veins. In November huge seed pods burst open to reveal orange berries hanging in clusters.

HABITAT: deep shade and will tolerate dry soil.
CONDITIONING: no special treatment. The leaves can be preserved either by the ironing or under carpet methods.

Pulmonaria
Many plants have spotted leaves which show well in a shady area. The flowers last well but the leaves are more difficult.
P. *augustifolia* 'Munstead Blue': one of my favourites. It has plain unspotted leaves. The flowers have pink buds that open up to a deep-blue on shorter stems than some varieties.
P. *officinalis*: spotted leaves. This best-known species of pulmonaria has pink buds which open up to tubular-shaped flowers that change from pink to blue.
P. *rubra*: coral-red flowers and spotless leaves.
P. *saccharata* 'Argentea': silver leaves that make a flat carpet on the ground.
P. 'Sissinghurst': white flowers.
We have given over a shady corner to pulmonaria.
HABITAT: humus, rich, retentive soil in continuing shade or semi-shade.
CONDITIONING: the leaves will last better if they are floated for an hour or two. Arrange the flowers in fairly deep water and they will last quite well.

Tellima
T. *grandiflora*: one of the best small shade-loving plants. In May the slim stems carry spines of pale-green bell-like flowers which gradually become tinged with pink. Very handsome leaves rather like an ivy leaf with serrated edges and strongly-marked veins.
T. G. 'rubra': an even better plant because it has rich pinky-red leaves.
HABITAT: sun or shade. It does well under trees but needs well-drained soil.
CONDITIONING: float the leaves in water for several hours.

Tiarella
T. *cordifolia*: a hardy perennial herb. The leaves are like a serrated ivy leaf with clearly defined veins. In the spring it has little cream flowers like a bottle brush.
HABITAT: shady or semi-shady. Will grow under trees.
CONDITIONING: float the leaves for several hours.

Vinca
V. *major* 'Variegata': I would not grow the dark-leaved variety as they make a shady corner very dark and dull. This variegated one is excellent. Long trailing stems are covered with oval variegated leaves that are invaluable in pedestals and large groups.
HABITAT: grows well in shade and any well-drained soils.
CONDITIONING: boiling water treatment essential and give long drink.

Viola

V. *labradorica*: excellent purple-flushed leaves. I pick them constantly to use in small arrangements.

HABITAT: dense shade.

CONDITIONING: no special treatment.

Zantedeschia

Z. *italicum* 'Pictum': beautiful arrow-shaped leaves that look like green marble. The leaves unfurl in October and continue to grow in size until May. By June the leaves have disappeared but in the autumn the stems bear clusters of scarlet berries which are poisonous.

HABITAT: sun or shade.

CONDITIONING: float leaves for an hour or so before arranging.

Grasses and grass-like plants

Grasses and plants resembling grass make unusual features both in the garden and for cutting. I have chosen several for colour and form. There are specialist nurseries which can provide a wide range including plants that thrive beside water.

Alopecurus

A. *pratensis* 'Aureus': this low-growing golden fox grass makes clumps of vividly-striped gold and green foliage. It has flower spikes growing up to about 20 in.

HABITAT: in front of any sunny border.

CONDITIONING: no special treatment.

Carex

C. *morrowii* 'Evergold': makes a useful low-growing clump with grass-like evergreen foliage. It is gold with narrow, green margin. The leaves make a good contrast to other darker ones.

HABITAT: in the front of a moist bed.

CONDITIONING: no special treatment.

Hakonechloa

H. *macra* 'Albo-aurea': a superb grass that all flower arrangers should have. It makes clumps of foliage about one ft high. Every ribbon-like leaf is variegated gold and buff with streaks of bronze.

HABITAT: well-drained soil, sun or semi-shade.

CONDITIONING: float the leaves for a short while before arranging.

Pennisetum

P. *alopecuroides*: a very attractive grass about two ft high. The long fluffy seed heads are pale pinkish-mauve. Dry well by the hang-dry method.

HABITAT: any well-drained soil. Sun or semi-shade.

Stipa

S. *arundinacea*: this is a spectacular grass two and a half ft high. In autumn the arching foliage is in every shade from buff through orange to browny-red. Long silky bronze seed heads complete the picture.

HABITAT: any good, well-drained soil.

CONDITIONING: dry the seed heads by the hang-dry method.

Ferns

Anyone with a semi-shady moist bit of ground can create a fernery. Ours is beside a dripping rain water butt. There are many nurseries specializing in ferns so that it is possible to make an interesting collection of large and small varieties. The following are just a few which I often use among other cut material.

Athyrium

A. *filix-femina*: known as the Lady Fern, probably because the fronds are delicate and light. It grows between one and four ft. It arranges well with small delicate flowers.

CONDITIONING: submerge the fronds for several hours in water. They dry well by the under carpet method.

Blechnum

B. *spicant* (*hard fern*): This small comb-like fern grows well in shady woodland areas. I have it in a peat bed and it does well. The little fronds dry well by the under carpet method and keep their colour. It grows to about nine in.

CONDITIONING: no special treatment.

Dryopteris

D. *filix-mas*: crisped fronds on either side of the stem taper at the bottom and the top. It grows well (up to three ft) and forms useful clumps.

CONDITIONING: float stems in water for at least an hour.

Phyllitis

P. *scolopendrium* (*hart's tongue*)

In Ireland, where it is common, it is known as the tongue of the wild boar. It grows well tucked in among stones and in semi-shady moist areas. The fronds, which grow to about one ft, are undivided, heart-shaped at the base and tapering at the tip. The shiny green leaves are very useful arranged among small flowers.

1. Mixed summer vase including delphinium, scabius, Enchantment lilies and roses.

2. *Eucalyptus gunnii symphoricarpus* and lilies in a Michael Leach jug.

3. (*Above right*) A wicker basket with its own lining filled with spring flowers including green *helleborus foetidus*, muscari and narcissus 'Geranium'. To the right of the picture is hebe foliage and left of centre a large leaf of *Arum italicum* 'Pictum'. The polyanthus and auriculas retained their roots and were tied inside plastic bags; after the flowers had died they were returned to the garden.

4. Single asters, fuchsia, roses, cosmos and lace-cap hydrangea with the pointed spires of *Polygonum affine*.

5. (*Above left*) Copper lustre jug filled with nasturtiums and marigolds.

6. Arrangement of mixed foliage including the pink autumn foliage of *Berberis thunbergii* 'Nana', together with *Alchemilla mollis*, *Stachys lanata* (rabbits' ears), hosta and white and purple grapes.

7. (*Above*) Pedestal workbox filled with roses, feverfew, philadelphus and *Alchemilla mollis*.

8. (*Above left*) Chestnut roaster with mixed foliage including *Vinca major* 'Variegata'; cotoneaster, pyracanthus 'Flava' and the dark brown dried seed heads of sisyrinchium.

9. A small urn arranged with small autumn flowers including white and mauve colchichum, *Polygonum affine*, geranium 'Buxton's Variety', *Salvia horminum* (clary), roses and fuchsia, with *Amaranthus caudatus viridis* falling over the front. This little urn fitted in well with the pattern of plates and cups.

10. Dried material arranged in a jug. It includes echinops (globe thistle); also *Molucella laevis* (bells of Ireland) and gypsophilia, both preserved by the glycerine method (hence the cream colour), hydrangea heads, achilla and *Stachys lanata* (rabbits' ears). In the front and low down are leaves of *Hedera canariensis* preserved by the under-carpet method.

11. (*Top*) A yellow marquee decorated with white trellis arches. These were outlined with yellow 'Enchantment' lilies, white spray chrysanthemums and trailing ivies (held in plastic bags and planted out afterwards), used together with yellow and green ribbon streamers and bows.

12. Dining room table decoration and candle-cup arrangements. The clashing red and pink flowers were chosen to set off the red wallpaper. The flowers included roses, dianthus and larkspur, with clusters of red cherries.

CONDITIONING: no special treatment.

Polystichum

P. *aculeatum*: decorative form of our native shield ferns. The fronds have a stiff leathery texture, glossy on top and matt underneath. Some fronds curve left and some right: this makes it particularly interesting. Grows well in semi-shady moist areas between one and two ft.

CONDITIONING: float for an hour before arranging.

Grey plants

Artemisia

There are many varieties which have grey foliage. Some are tender and most of them are perennial. They prefer parched soils and good drainage, but I have found several which do well on heavy clay.

A. *absinthium* 'Lambrook Silver': shrub with bold-cut leaves.

A. × 'Powis Castle': hardy spreading shrub with pinnate grey foliage.

HABITAT: sunny position. Well-drained soil.

A. *arborescens*: silver filigree foliage. Quick growing but tender.

HABITAT: warm, sunny position. well-drained soil.

A. *ludoviciana*: my favourite grey plant. Perennial. Grows like a weed. Pretty, willow-like leaves and very silvery flowers extending up to a pointed top. Dries well by the hang-dry method.

HABITAT: seeds itself everywhere. Sun or shade, in any soil.

A. *stelleriana*: almost white in colour with large felted chrysanthemum-like leaves.

HABITAT: good edging for a sunny well-drained border.

CONDITIONING: all artemisia plants need boiling water treatment. The stems must have their ends hammered and then be given a long drink. When leaves alone are used, float them for a few minutes.

Ballota

B. *pseudodictamnus*: a hardy perennial. From a woody base spring long curved stems covered in apple green leaves that gradually become white.

HABITAT: dry, well-drained soil, sunny or semi-shady position.

CONDITIONING: give boiling water treatment and a long drink.

Hebe

H. *pineloides* 'Quick Silver': small evergreen shrub with blue-grey leaves and blue flowers in summer.

H. *pinguifolia* 'Pagei': low-growing plant with glaucous foliage and white flowers in May.

HABITAT: sunny position, well-drained soil.

CONDITIONING: split ends and give good drink.

Helichrysum

H. *petiolatum*: a superb foliage plant. The long arching stems are covered with tiny grey leaves. Very suitable for tubs and pots and as a border plant. I like to cut long stems to cascade over the edge of large pedestal groups.

HABITAT: dry sunny position and most soils.

CONDITIONING: hammer ends. Long drink.

Santolina

S. *chamaecyparissus*: dense bushes of silver-grey feathery foliage. Small yellow button flowers in July which I often use separately in bridesmaids' headdresses and Victorian posies.

HABITAT: sun and good drainage.

CONDITIONING: hammer ends. Long drink.

Senecio

There are hundreds of species of senecio, many of them with excellent grey foliage.

S. *cineria* 'White Diamond': grey diamond-shaped leaves.

S. *cineria* 'Ramparts': deeply-cut foliage.

HABITAT: sunny position and poor soil.

CONDITIONING: hammer ends and give boiling water treatment.

S. *greyii*. Roy Lancaster has renamed this shrub 'Sunshine', which is now officially accepted. It is one of the most popular, with its grey-green leaves and almost white underleaf. It has small yellow flowers.

HABITAT: prefers sun, otherwise it will straggle into an untidy woody shrub.

CONDITIONING: hammer ends and give long drink. It will preserve by the hang-dry method.

Stachys

S. *lanata* (*lamb's lug*): large felted grey leaves from which spring grey spines covered in pink flowers. The leaves can be used individually. The spines dry well (see page 99).

S. *lanata* 'Sheila Macqueen': being the namesake of such a distinguished flower arranger and gardener, one would expect this to be special – and it is!

HABITAT: sun or shade.

CONDITIONING: hammer ends and give long drink.

2. Flowers and colours

Blue

A pure blue flower is rare. What the gardening catalogues call blue often turns out to be related colours in the mauve and purple range. A real true blue comes in various forms. There is that misty, hazy blue found in woods after rain which turns out to be glades of bluebells. There is also that piercing gentian blue. Cluny Garden near Aberfeldy in Perthshire has a magnificent collection of rare shrubs and trees. But in late summer the most dazzling sight of all, even before one reaches the main part of the garden, is a carpet of deep blue gentians. There is also that unique blue Tibetan poppy *Meconopsis baileyi*. It stands straight and tall bearing miraculous crinkly-edged translucent petals. We first saw it at the garden at Inverewe, which now belongs to the National Trust for Scotland, rising up from beds of cream and apricot azaleas – an unforgettable sight and a combination of colours which I have often used in flower arrangements. One has, however, to face the fact that these special poppies need a lime-free peaty soil and so are not suitable for many gardens.

One obvious blue flower for summer bedding and a joy to the flower arranger is the delphinium, which comes in many shades. Even a small garden will have room for one or two clumps, ranging from deep blue to pale. There are excellent campanulas, which sow themselves year after year, and nigella is a useful flower. Anchusa, as I have only recently discovered, lasts very well when cut and seeds itself like mad. It needs to be massed to make any impact, so as soon as the seedlings appear re-plant as many as you need in groups and ruthlessly throw out the rest. Massed together they become pools of deep blue. Left on their own they form untidy nondescript little blots. There is, of course, a good range of blue hydrangea, including lace cap varieties. The mop-heads abound in seaside areas and have a spectacular blue range. They need an acid soil.

A very useful lily, agapanthus, is one of the most clear blue flowers. Its lovely round head stands above spear-shaped leaves. I have mine in a pot which I bring into the house for special parties. There is a good, new hardy one, Headbourne hybrid, which is one of the smaller varieties and looks very well in mixed borders. It is wonderful as a cut flower.

Much as I love blue flowers in summer and autumn, my favourite time is the spring, when grape hyacinths and miniature irises mingle in the beds with primroses and other small flowers. The new spring foliages make a good background and help to provide a continual source of little posies for the house.

There are many excellent blue clematis flowering throughout the summer from the little lantern macropetala to the large single jackmanii. We have a jackmanii which romps through the rose *Zepherine Drouhin*; the marvellous bright pink of the rose makes a good contrast.

2 Miniature arrangement of *Iris reticulata*, *Primula vulgaris* (primrose), snowdrops and ivy leaves

Blue cut flowers must have natural light. What looks brilliant in the garden will be grey and dreary under electric light. A light room does, however, make a superb background for blue. White walls are excellent, also apricot. Pale yellow and limey-green also give attractive contrasts for blue groups. Variegated foliages like *Vinca major*, eleagnus and the versatile alchemilla also contrast well. A basket filled with massed cornflowers or grape hyacinths placed on a scrubbed kitchen table is a great favourite.

The average garden centre supplies a very limited range of interesting blue plant material. I have bought many of my special treasures from plant stalls at gardens which are open to the public or specialist nurseries which exhibit at the Royal Horticultural Society's shows at Vincent Square.

Brown

Brown is at the very heart of a garden – earth, branches and the differing shades of brick and stone – and this is particularly so in late autumn. Our garden is typical of many in this season with stretches of earth already cleared and planted with bulbs and a few brightly-coloured leaves still clinging to otherwise bare trees and shrubs. Apart from a few late flowering roses and viburnums the garden colour is predominantly green and brown, green from the evergreen shrubs and brown from the earth and trees. A month ago it was a very different picture – bright autumn flowers contrasting with the many splendid seed heads ranging in colour from sage green to beige and brown.

Autumn produces some brown flowers, like zinnias, which include brown among the yellows and reds, and rudbeckia, one variety of which, called Rustic, has splendid mahogany-coloured blooms. *Rudbeckia fulgida* has bright yellow petals encircling deep brown cone-like heads. When the petals fall the cones remain with a frill of bright green leaves and make a charming addition to posies of autumn flowers. Once the leaves fall the seed heads dry well. Among the many other plants which produce good seed heads sisyrinchum gives a particularly good dark brown variety and the stem changes to the same colour. I used it in the chestnut roaster (see colour pl. 8) to add interest to the variegated green.

Copper beech is the obvious brown autumn foliage for large mixed groups in house or church. It is very effective if used with discretion. So often flower arrangers use it with such abandon that all other colours are lost. Branches used sparingly and carefully placed are invaluable in giving shape to a large arrangement, but if they are used as very solid background foliage the effect is at once overpowering and heavy. Avoid using copper beech against dark panelling: the result is disastrous.

Some plant material which is preserved by the glycerine method changes to deep brown and one or two branches of single leaves give a good strong tone to mixed autumn groups.

In the spring, wallflowers blossom forth in many shades of brown. They are in fact the only wholly brown flowers at this season which I can recollect. There are, however, attractive hellebores with brown and cream or green markings, and later there are parrot tulips with the same colouring.

In early summer there are no obvious brown garden flowers, but many which have attractive brown markings. There are two particularly good lilies; *Lilium brownii*, cream-backed with brown, which makes it very interesting for flower arrangers, and *Lilium auratum*, the beautiful cream trumpet of which has definite brown markings. Later in the summer sedum (stonecrop) appears in many forms including one variety with brown stem and leaves and a buff-coloured flower. We plant it in our garden grouped together to create a strong contrast with other lighter varieties and variegated shrubs. I use it in the same way for house and church flowers and it also dries well.

In winter I often cut a branch from an apple tree. It must be an interesting shape, preferably with one or two curving twigs. I place the branch in an ordinary earthenware flower pot filled with soil, rammed well down so that the branch, when pushed right into it, is held steady. I wire on sprays of everlasting flowers. The white daisy-like variety looks very good against the brown bark. I then add sprays of honesty. When the outer brownish layers of the seed case are peeled off the transparent silvery centres are revealed, looking like translucent leaves. I have the 'tree ' in front of a looking-glass in an alcove in the dining-room with well-hidden lighting and the effect is very fairy-like and pretty.

Green

During the last 20 years there has been an increased interest in green and variegated foliage plants, perhaps attributable to flower arrangers? The great achievement of flower clubs is that they have trained our eyes to look for special form, texture and colour, not necessarily restricted to flowering plants but often provided by interesting foliage and seed heads. What might once have ended in the wheelbarrow is now nurtured as an important part of a green group. Beautifully shaped buds are as important in their green stage as when they burst into flower.

As a result of this new interest the country abounds in nurseries specializing in foliage plants, not only evergreens but also variegated and those that have spectacular and vivid autumn colours. The moment a new green or variegated plant becomes fashionable it is swept up rapturously by eager flower arrangers.

The smallest garden can provide a wide range of good green plant material. From January right through to the spring there are many excellent hellebores. One of my favourites is Helleborus foetidus. From dark green finger-like leaves spring pale stems bearing flowers which hang like little green cups.

Euphorbia is another green plant essential to the flower arranger. Euphorbia wulfenii, one of the largest, has very striking thickish brown-scaled stems leading up to huge heads of green disc-like flowers. In a small garden it takes up quite a lot of space but is well worth it. It provides height both to the garden bed and to flower groups. A smaller variety is Euphorbia robbiae. Very dark rosettes of small green leaves break into charming pale greeny-yellow heads which flower in May and June. This euphorbia quickly develops into a ground cover and needs to be well controlled! There are many more euphorbias listed on page 15.

One of the most spectacular leaves for spring groups is that of Arum italicum pictum. The surface of the plant's unique arrow-shaped leaves has the appearance of green and cream marble. These arums flourish in shaded areas. Mine have increased in size since I dug in a quantity of peat and leafmould, having initially planted them in a deep hole filled with vegetable compost.

These leaves add interest to any flower arrangement.

In designing your garden it is a good idea to include what are sometimes called 'architectural' plants – that is, plants which have a regular outline, such as *Iris foetidissima variegata* and phormium. Both these plants have clearly marked strap-like leaves which give shape and interest to many flower arrangements. Phormium comes in a wide range of cream and green. (There is also a red and pink variety.)

As spring merges into summer, that flower arranger's delight, *Alchemilla mollis*, abounds. Make sure that it does not become too rampant. Take off the dead heads or cut it and hang it up for drying the moment the flowers begin to fade – otherwise it will seed itself and overtake your next year's planting. It has very pretty, large rounded, green leaves, which when picked and used separately are useful for mixed posies. The flower itself is a joy: fluffy limey-green heads on long slender stems. I use it constantly, both in vases and in garlands. At an early summer church flower festival we have hung on to the pew ends polythene bags containing wet Oasis and surrounded by chicken wire into which we pushed short stems of alchemilla. The effect of the alchemilla running the whole length of the pews on either side of the nave was of a green path leading up to the chancel flowers, a very pretty cool contrast to other strong colours.

Viburnum opulus sterile is a great joy at the end of May. The branches bear balls of light green, tiny flowers which look enchanting in mixed green groups, especially if the stems are fairly heavily de-leafed so that the balls stand out clearly.

Solomon's seal (*Polygonatum multiflorum*) is another late spring treasure. The greenish white bell-like flowers hang down from arching stems of dark green leaves, so adding a special shape to large green groups. A useful feature of this plant is that it flowers in shaded areas.

A good flower arrangement needs clearly defined leaves with shapes that stand out well against other foliage and flowers. The hosta provides exactly that. Hosta 'Thomas Hogg' is one of the best. It has excellent well-shaped pointed leaves with creamy margins. While many hostas have uninteresting flowers, this one is exceptional in having tall, mauve, trumpet-like flowers which are almost as decorative as the leaves. *Hosta sieboldiana* has much larger blue green leaves which make it a popular choice for large flower arrangements. There is in fact a very wide choice of hostas, many of which have small beautifully marked leaves. Those listed on page 37 are the most useful. Hostas need to be constantly protected from slugs. Guarding them is a laborious job but well worth the effort involved.

There are several good green flowers which owe their popularity to flower arrangers. Amongst these are nicotiana 'Limelight', a good green variety, and (one which was new to me) *Nicotiana langsdorffii*, an enchanting variety which has tiny green trumpet-like flowers with a delicate habit of growth.

Another wonderful plant which I think can legitimately be included in the green range is astrantia. The stem bears a cluster of small flowers resembling tiny posies, some creamy green, some flushed with pink. One of the most beautiful is *Astrantia major* 'Shaggy'. It has larger flowers than most varieties, cream tipped with an acid green. Another, *Astrantia major* 'Sunningdale Variegated', is superb. The green flowers have pink centres, and the leaves are bright green edged with cream.

There is, of course, a lovely range of mixed ivies to add interest and shape to many vases. One of these, a mixture of a fatsia and an ivy, *fatshedera* 'Variegata', is a splendid climber. The leaves are ivy-shaped but gain substance from the fact that they are more fleshy in appearance, like the leaves of all fatsias. The stems are pink and the leaves have clear creamy markings with splashes of pink on a green background. Another good green climber is *Cobaea scandens*. It starts off with a cream trumpet-like flower which gradually changes to green. It is easily grown from seed as an annual.

There are so many shrubs that provide perfect green foliage that it is difficult to single out individual ones, but camellia, skimmia, fatsia and variegated examples like eleagnus and euonymus spring more readily to mind than most. I have mentioned special leaves for green groups, but for little posies it is the ground covers which come into their own. Tellima, lamium and cyclamen leaves make enchanting foliage posies.

Autumn gives the gardener a chance to see whether the greens are setting off other colours as they should. A dark corner may well need lighting with a variegated or yellow leaved shrub; a grey plant may be lost unless it is planted against a good contrasting neighbour, and red and yellow autumn colours easily disappear among an excess of dark evergreens.

To obtain the right effect it may be desirable to move plants and shrubs. My own experience is that most will move at any time except in very cold weather provided that a large hole is dug in the new site and filled with water and the plant or shrub is moved immediately. I then continue to water, if necessary twice a day, using a hose if it is a mature specimen so that the leaves are thoroughly soaked, until I am quite sure that it has established itself in its new abode.

In high summer a green group arranged against a white or pale-coloured wall will create a cool and calm atmosphere. In July the lime trees (tilia) are showing enchanting pale green bracts and fluffy green flowers. If the branches are stripped of all leaves the bracts and flowers will stand out and make a simple green arrangement, especially if the vase is placed in natural light to capture the delicacy of the flowers.

The dining-room table decorations shown in the colour section are splendid in the winter but could be too overpowering on a summer's evening. Instead the candle cups arranged with variegated ivies and the central dish filled with green grapes, peppers and vine leaves give a cool and pretty effect.

Green arrangements need to have a strong central point. This is often achieved by using three or five clearly defined single leaves like hosta or *Arum italicum.* In the illustration on colour pl. 6, which is a mixture of different foliages, grapes have been used instead of leaves to give added interest and a different shiny texture.

In dealing with the preservation of plant material in chapter 5 I have suggested collecting coloured leaves to preserve them. These mix very well with fresh evergreen plant material and help to make a winter green group more interesting.

Grey

During the last 20 years flower arrangers have come to appreciate the importance of grey foliage and nowadays there are several excellent nurseries which specialize in providing it. I think that the use of grey and white in famous gardens, often effectively mixed with pale colours or used as a foil to bright scarlets and yellows, has had a considerable influence and produced a great demand for grey and silver plants.

Do remember, however, that many grey foliage plants are tender. Furthermore, all of them need very good drainage. A very grand nurseryman looked despairingly when I asked him exactly what he meant by 'good drainage'. 'Obviously, Madam,' he replied, 'I mean that there must not be any pools of water lying on the surface.' He did eventually concede that there could be drainage problems without water being apparent, in which case it is a great help if, when a hole is dug for a new plant, a mixture of grit and sand is placed at the bottom.

A particularly good grey plant is *Artemisia ludoviciana*, which thrives in my garden in sun or shade. It grows to about one and a half feet and has pointed, willowy, silvery grey leaves. It is laden in summer with silvery flowers that are not very interesting except that they dry well by the hang-dry method and make a nice pointed shape for dried groups. It lasts well indoors and consequently I often use it in tubs. The little grey seedlings can also be replanted to form good grey blocks in the garden.

Grey like blue and mauve is a colour that can be disappointing when cut unless it stands in natural light, in which case it mixes well with, for example, scabious and delphinium. Grey is good with red and yellow in the house as well as in the garden.

The range of grey plants is enormous and I advise sending for a catalogue from a specialist nursery, but on page 59 is a list of plants that I constantly use, both for large arrangements and for small ones.

Mauve and purple

Mauve and purple cut flowers are not easy to arrange because they need natural light. Placed near a window against a pale background the colouring is good; for instance, a large urn filled with every shade of mauve and purple delphinium is a rich and wonderful sight. In a simpler way a silver bowl massed with sweet peas in these colours is glorious, provided that it is placed in a room with natural light; otherwise the mauves and purples become grey and drab. They can, however, be lifted up by additions of bright variegated foliage and touches of magenta pink. I learned this some years ago when visiting the National Trust garden at Ascott House near Wing. So often herbaceous borders are simply a mixture of bright colours planted without any obvious overall planning. This border (designed by Barbara Oakley) was an exception and one of the most beautiful that I have seen. It was an object lesson in clever planting, and it taught me so much about mauve and purple as colours both for flower arranging and in a garden that I shall describe it in some detail.

The basic plan consisted of two borders running either side of a long path, one side flanked by a wall of soft-coloured brick topped by variegated hollies, the other backed by yellowish yews. This yellow and variegated colouring made an original background to what at first appeared to be mauve and purple borders. Had these been the only colours they would have been very drab at any time except under bright sunlight, but the mauves and purples were in fact lifted by splashes of bright magenta pink, variegated greens, clumps of lime green nicotiana, *Alchemilla mollis*, pale pinks and white.

The wall had many superb climbing plants including a lovely perennial mauve pea, and various clematis, amongst them 'Perle d'Azure', which is a very pretty pale-mauve, and *Romneya coulteri*, which has glorious huge white flowers with bright-yellow stamens. These climbers grew high up the wall. All of them last well as cut flowers. The roses in the beds were mostly of the small shrub varieties in pale and subtle colours, like 'Gruss an Aachen', a pale-pinky-cream, and 'Silver Charm', a pale-mauve.

Among the taller flowers (which incidentally make excellent backing for large groups) were various Michaelmas daisies ranging in colour from pale-mauve to deep-purple, and thalictrum; its purple flowers do not last well in water, but its foliage does, and is very pretty and light. *Thalictrum glaucum* has bluey-grey leaves which are useful tall material as the plant grows to about five feet. The smaller flowers and foliage included clumps of purple and mauve pansies and petunias, together with that flower arranger's favourite, pentstemon ('Sour Grapes'). Down the length of both borders clumps of mauve gypsophila were planted at intervals. Deep-mauve foliage was provided by the sage *Salvia 'Tricolour'*, again good solid clumps of it at regular intervals. The colour fades into yellowish-pinky shades as the plant matures. Little sprigs of this cut for summer and autumn posies are very useful.

One of the best flowers in these borders from the flower arranger's point of view was a spectacular phlox, 'Hampton Court', which is a lovely clear mauve with large flowers. Throughout there were groups of *Lilium candidum* and *Allium christophii*. Both the lilies and the allium cut well. The latter has lovely large pale-mauve heads on tall stems which produce good seed heads for drying.

In the past I had only used verbena in tubs and window-boxes, but since seeing it as a bright-pink contrast to this predominantly mauve border I now use it as a bedding plant. It goes on flowering right through the summer and autumn. In fact, although it is tender, I have had it at Christmas, and it lasts extremely well in water. 'Rose' is a good bright-pink variety.

The border at Ascott brought home to me the importance of having variegated and coloured foliage plants. The variegated holly growing over the wall set the scene. A flower arranger needs a constant source of shrubs and plants with coloured leaves. One such is *Euonymus fortunei* 'Gracilis' which, because it clings and grows so well on walls produces long curving sprays of green edged with cream and makes a perfect contrast to a few stems of mauve sweet peas.

I am always searching for long slim vases for this sort of arrangement and I have found two or three Edwardian trumpet-shaped ones that are perfect. The trailing foliage falls over the edge and the taller stems stand up well behind. A tall vase like this is excellent for sprays of mauve clematis mixed with variegated foliage. The clematis sits down well into the trumpet and the flowers fall naturally over the edge.

I find botanical names very hard to remember. I still talk firmly of lilac and not as the purists do of syringa. Call it what you will, it is an excellent shrub for flower arrangers and there are dwarf varieties – not all that dwarf in my experience, but smaller than some. The shrub – or in some cases small tree – has superb panicles of every shade from white through pink and pale mauve to deep purple. Massed together, stripped of most of the leaves, they provide superb material for the flower arranger. 'Charles X' has single pale mauve tresses and 'Massena' is deep reddish purple with large tresses. Among the most spectacular double varieties is 'General Pershing', which is a particularly deep violet purple and gives depth to any mauve and purple group.

Orange

Orange, being a mixture of red and yellow, is a very penetrating colour. A long border in a large garden can take clumps of solid orange or orange and yellow and they have an eye-catching quality which is exciting and important. The problem in a small garden is that such a vibrant colour tends to overpower other planting. For instance, I had a tub planted with variegated ivies and orange enchantment lilies which I liked. I had, however, forgotten that the tub stood in front of a wall covered with the rose *Zepherine Drouhin*. The bright magenta pink of the rose spelt death to the orange lilies. With no paler plants in between the contrast was too strong and sudden.

In spring and summer it is not easy to achieve a pure orange group. Iceland poppies, for instance, spring from mixed seeds, a lovely colour range which includes salmon pink, pale apricot and orange. One ligtu variety of alstromeria again has a great mixture of pinks leading into deep orange. Polyanthus are always sold in mixed boxes or seed packets; but they can be easily split in the autumn and the orange plants separated for future planting.

One of the most beautiful orange flowers is the Crown Imperial (*Fritillaria imperialis*), a perfect flower both for the garden and for the flower arranger. One of the many euphorbias, *Euphorbia griffithi* (fine glow), makes a very good orange cushion embedded in its own bright green leaves.

In a small garden I prefer orange used sparingly with pale apricot and cream. Azaleas are the perfect example. Blue is a good contrast to these colours and azaleas underplanted with bluebells make a wonderful sight.

One of the most striking herbaceous perennials is eremurus, which has wonderful tall spikes covered in small flowers, rather like an up-market lupin! It comes in many different pink, cream, red and yellow shades, but the best for a small garden is *Eremurus bungei*, which is a marvellous orange and smaller than the other varieties. It is favoured highly by flower arrangers because the tall spikes give height and interest to any large group.

Later in the year orange provides a very important part of our autumn colouring. Almost overnight leaves turn from green through orange to deep red. Cotoneaster and berberis in particular give constantly changing leaf colour, and they are a source of superb berries. Pyracantha (firethorn) is, however, perhaps the most vivid of the orange-berried shrubs. Autumn compels flower arrangers to work on a large canvas. It is hard to restrict vases to little posies when there is such an abundance of material waiting to be cut.

In the autumn crocosmia (monbretia) is a very useful plant. The rather boring monbretia seen endlessly in the gardens of little seaside villas should in my view be replaced by *Crocosmia masonorum*. This is a much better plant with bright reddish-orange star-like flowers. The stems arch over so that the flowers face upwards, which is a great advantage from the flower arranger's point of view. This variety has long strap-like leaves which dry well. Crocosmia 'Emily McKenzie' flowers from August to October. It has very impressive orange and mahogany-coloured flowers which add enormously to autumn groups. Another good tall orange spiky flower is *Kniphofia galpinii*, an orange red-hot poker. A stem or two of either of these plants gives a pointed shape that provides contrast to the rounded flowers of dahlias and zinnias and that excellent autumn flower rudbeckia.

Bright autumn colours are a sensational contrast against dark panelling or green or pale mushroom-coloured walls.

While autumn provides the opportunity for large groups of foliage and berries it is also very satisfying to pick bunches of marigolds and to arrange them on their own in a copper bowl. They look splendid on a dark wooden table or chest or any bright-coloured cloth. Another favourite, easily grown flower is the common nasturtium (tropaeolum). I like to include a variety which has variegated leaves and both the upright and trailing forms. The buds will continue to open in water, which makes it a very useful flower arranger's plant. Nowadays there is an excellent colour range, from pale cream through to apricot as well as bright orange and red. I often arrange nasturtiums in a copper lustre mug. The dark shiny surface reflects the different colours (see colour pl. 5).

Pink

If I were in the dreadful – if unlikely! – position of being allowed only one colour in a garden I think that I would choose pink. To the flower arranger it gives a vast range of colour, starting off from the palest shade and going right through to Magenta dianthus. Pink starts for me with camellia. Where else can one find a shrub that gives so much – all those glorious pink and red flowers of every conceivable shade set in that ravishing shiny green foliage? I hardly dare suggest that it gives us much more than the rhododendron. Of course, in a big garden, glades and hedges of rhododendron are a marvellous sight: but in a small garden where space is limited camellia gives much better value. Once rhododendron is over the flower arranger is left with nothing but boring dark green foliage, so different from the dark glossy leaves of the camellia, which will last for up to six weeks in water. The japonica variety thrives on pruning, so there need be no guilty feelings when sprays are cut for the house.

There are very many other good pink flowering shrubs which last well in water, including viburnums, roses, escalonia (the variety called 'Apple Blossom'), and of course prunus in its different forms. In a small garden, however, I would not grow prunus for flower arranging, because its season is too short and its foliage is not sufficiently interesting. The only exception which I would make is the miraculous winter-flowering *Prunus subhirtella autumnalis*. Its branches are covered with tiny, star-like flowers. Officially it is white, but I find that massed together in a flower arrangement it takes on a faint pink tone because the flowers have tiny clusters of pinky-yellow stamens. I have often used it in this way in church for winter weddings.

Roses provide a great range of pink tones. Climbers and the miniature fairy roses are the varieties best suited to a small garden, because shrubs take up too much space.

The flower arranger has an enormous choice of pink annuals and perennials. It is hard to know where to start when talking about them. Dianthus has a very wide range and lasts well in water, particularly if the flowers are kept dead-headed. They will continue to open for several weeks. 'Doris' is a top favourite, a good clear peachy pink, widely sold in shops because it travels and lasts well. Flower arrangers need material which varies in height and shape. Antirrhinum (snapdragon) and digitalis (foxglove) give a much needed pointed shape to mixed groups and grow easily. There is a new variety of antirrhinum, 'Butterfly', which has particularly large blossoms. It is very effective for flower arrangements.

Penstemons are another favourite. They remind me of tiny foxgloves. They are tender and, unless grown in a warm area, have to be treated as biennials. *Phlox paniculata* is an excellent garden and flower arranger's plant, with lovely bright pink heads on tall stems. All these flowers make a splendid summer group, either on their own or mixed with cascades of philadelphus stripped of its leaves and white lilies to give greater height.

Pink flowers stand out well against most backgrounds. White and green walls provide good contrasts and so, rather surprisingly, do red walls, provided that some of the pink tones in with the red.

Autumn flower arrangements tend to contain orange, yellow and brown colours, but one of my favourite autumn flowers is the *Nerine bowdenii*, a superb pink lily, coming originally from Guernsey – not Jersey as some islanders claim. It grows well against sunny walls and it increases slowly, provided that it is not moved. The bulbs seem to enjoy being overcrowded.

A friend's garden in Orkney disobeys all the rules because there nerines flourish on a north-facing windy ridge. The long pale green strap-like leaves appear first and then the flowers, clusters of tiny trumpets on tall pinky-green stems, superb in mixed groups with variegated or grey foliage or mixed with autumn flowering vibernum and late roses. Nerines last well in water and flower for several weeks in the garden.

As pink harmonizes so well with many different colours flower arrangers would do well to make it a top priority when choosing bedding plants and flowering shrubs.

Red

Red conjures up different pictures to different people. Some gardeners and flower arrangers find it dominant, exhausting, and overpowering, and prefer pale subtle colours. Again these appear wishy-washy, boring, and inspid to other eyes. I feel that each colour range has its own particular quality, and depends almost always on background and location. If one colour is used on its own the flowers must include different shades, different textures and different shapes and heights.

Flower arrangers have come to use the term 'a clashing red group'. What they mean by that rather ambiguous expression is a vase arranged not only with every shade of red and pink, light and dark, but also all those colours from orange to purple which include red. This may sound horrendous to the uninitiated, but in fact these colours are very dramatic when used together. To give the right effect, however, the various shades must be grouped correctly. The light and the dark colours hold the eye and therefore dictate the shape of the arrangement. Pale pinks give a good outline to the vase and should gradually merge into oranges, reds and purples, which between them give emphasis and depth. If the different colours are spattered about indiscriminately there will be no good overall shape.

The same strong colours grouped together in garden borders give great interest. When using clashing reds in a border it is important not to plant indiscriminately, because if you do you will find that the border loses its shape. One method of planting is to distribute your blocks of colour fairly evenly throughout the length of the border. An alternative method, which can be very effective in a small garden, is to start with bright reds at one end and then shade off into pale colours at the other. Hidcote Manor has a wonderful garden now maintained by the National Trust. Within the main garden there is a red garden, enclosed by grey walls. I stood amazed by the brilliant collection of mixed reds which included bright red dahlias, clematis, roses, phlox and, of course, that jewel among red perennials – *Lobelia cardinalis*. This plant has marvellous spikes of red flowers with deep dark red foliage. Among the foliage plants I remember particularly a spectacular red-leafed phormium.

Clashing reds look splendid against dark panelling, and against green, red or pink walls; but I think that they are inartistic when placed against a clear white wall. The contrast is too strong. In the dining-room table decorations shown in colour pl. 12 this colouring worked well against our red walls. Green takes away the impact of a red arrangement. As you see, no foliage was added to these table decorations. The red cherries added a different texture to the flowers. Red peppers or even tomatoes can often be included.

There are many varieties of red flowers which look excellent on their own or with special foliage; for example, scarlet carnations with grey foliage. That fine kaffir lily schizostylis stands well with a few small autumn-coloured paeony leaves. Bowls of red anemones massed together look marvellous on a bright blue or green linen cloth.

Our English country churches are inclined to look cold and very often are cold! Red flowers do help to give a feeling of warmth. I always encourage brides who are being married in the winter to choose warm colours for the bridesmaids. Apricot shades or reds or deep pinks can have matching flowers which all help to create a warm atmosphere – even if it is often only an illusion of warmth!

White and cream

I consider white and cream together because it is very difficult to find a pure white flower as any florist who has endeavoured to make an all white bouquet for a dead white bridal dress will confirm! Against it the bouquet will appear either yellow or else greenish white.

There must be many people in England who, like me, first saw a white border at Sissinghurst. I was completely bowled over by the purity and perfection of the planting. Reading Victoria Glendenning's book, *Vita*, in which the writer tells in detail of the ideas behind this part of the Sissinghurst garden, I was interested to learn that originally Vita Sackville-West wanted to combine some pink with the white border; but her husband, Harold Nicholson, insisted on using only grey as a contrast. How right he was! Grey provides a soft and subtle contrast to the purity and translucence of white flowers, whether growing in the garden or picked for the house. Much as I would like to create an all white and grey border, I know that there is not room for it in our small garden, though white does predominate in our summer planting.

White like dark colours holds the eye: therefore in gardens as in mixed flower arrangements it needs to be placed carefully. In the case both of arrangements and of garden beds it must be used so as to give shape and form, not scattered at random, so becoming shapeless and dull.

Personally I like to see white and cream blend gradually into deeper colours. Both in garden planting and when I am planning a vase of flowers I aim to use it as a spectacular contrast with blue or pale apricot. What I detest is to see white against dark red: the contrast is too strong and sudden.

A flower bed which includes white flowers can be given extra height by means of white climbers. A climbing 'Iceberg' rose makes a spectacular background, and two varieties of clematis, 'Henryi' and 'Marie Boisselot', are almost pure white. These look wonderful when mixed with other pale colours.

When it comes to decorating in the house or church white flowers are again superb. Although one might imagine that white flowers in a white room would be dull, in fact they are elegant and beautiful. Most white flowers, particularly lilies, have a translucent quality, the more so if the vase is arranged and placed so that the light comes through them. Then the different shades which one finds in white flowers become more apparent.

A mixed white arrangement needs flowers of different shapes and textures. When flowers that taper like white foxgloves (digitalis) and delphiniums are mixed with roses a more rounded form results. Sprays of double and single philadelphus stripped of its leaves combined perhaps with the white *Lilium martagon* (the Turk's cap lily) and a stem or two of *Lilium candidum* (Madonna lily), which immediately give a different dimension, are spectacular whether for a pedestal in church or for a formal drawing-room.

In late summer and autumn there is an outstanding shrub – symphoricarpus (snowberry). The long arching sprays bear clusters of shiny white berries which are a perfect foil to stiffer and more formal lilies (see colour pl. 2). I use it too with the pink Guernsey lily, *Nerine bowdenii*, and mixed grey foliage. The symphoricarpus does, however, take up a good deal of space and if it is planted too near to other shrubs it will not berry so profusely.

Daisies (which are in fact chrysanthemums) in all their various forms are excellent and flower for ages. They will mix well with other summer flowers, but also look well on their own massed in baskets or bowls. Feverfew, one of the pyrethrum section of chrysanthemums, is very useful, extremely prolific, and

3 Favourite lilies:
A: *Lilium speciosum rubrum*
B: *Lilium auratum*
C: *Lilium regale*
D: *Nerine bowdenii*
E: *Lilium* 'Enchantment'

nearly always in bloom. Indeed, it grows like a weed and has to be firmly controlled. Each stem branches out bearing clusters of tiny white flowers with yellow centres. It is useful for garlands and small posies. A tall autumn-flowering white daisy is *Chrysanthemum uliginosum*, which is excellent for the house or church. *Chrysanthemum maximum* 'Esther Read' is a double daisy which lasts very well, but I find it rather unattractive in the garden, so I am gradually eliminating it!

Among the smaller low-growing white plants which are especially useful for picking is *Dianthus allwoodii*, mixed either with the pink variety or on its own with grey foliage. One of the best is a hybrid, 'Hayter', the flowers of which are almost as big as those of the carnation and last well when cut.

My favourite of all white flowers is the lily of the valley (*Convallaria majalis*). I have a glass bowl which fits into a silver coaster into which I mass the exquisite bell-like lilies surrounded by a frill of their own leaves, thus making a perfect table decoration.

There are many white flowering shrubs. Philadelphus 'Belle Etoile' is one of my favourites, a marvellous off-white single flower with a pink centre. It needs to be stripped of its leaves so that the flowers stand out. They look superb arranged on their own or mixed with other flowers. Colour pl. 7 shows philadelphus arranged with roses in a pedestal work-box. Syringa, another good white-flowered shrub, must be stripped of most of its leaves as otherwise the blossoms will not last well in water.

Yellow

Yellow is a very important colour both for gardeners and for flower arrangers. It is with us throughout the year, even in the bleakest of weather, giving a sense of sunshine and lightness to the darkest corner. Yellow winter-flowering shrubs are a great bonus and one of the best is the winter-flowering jasmine (*jasminum nudiflorum*) with bare branches covered in small star-like yellow flowers. It can be trained against sunny walls or fences, where it will flower profusely from December to February. I use it in the house at Christmas mixed with variegated holly and ivy leaves.

There are two yellow-flowered shrubs which pre-empt spring. One is the winter-flowering witch hazel (*hamamelis mollis*), an unusual shrub with dark branches from which appear strange spidery flowers. A stem or two cut for the house is a great joy on a winter's day. A warm room will soon bring out the strong scent, which might be missed outside. The other is corylopsis, which flowers in February. I first saw it several years ago at the February show of the Royal Horticultural Society at Vincent Square and was very impressed. It has long arching stems covered with small spiky flowers that make it one of the best of shrubs for the flower arranger. I like it arranged on its own or mixed with other early spring flowers and trailing ivies. It is rather tender, but I would try to include it even in a cold garden. If it is planted in a sheltered corner it will survive the winter even though flowering less profusely.

Forsythia is another useful shrub; for example, for a winter party in the house or a special occasion in church. Its long sprays covered in yellow blossom stand out well. It has the advantage that it can be cut in tight bud and brought into the warmth where it will open in two to three weeks.

Yellow is particularly associated with spring. Drifts of crocuses and daffodils, clumps of pale primroses and vivid polyanthus provide a heart-warming sight, especially on a day which is cold and bleak! The garden should at this time provide lots of flowers for picking. Some flowers are more difficult to arrange than others. Thus daffodils are inclined to be stiff and disappointing when cut and arranged in large vases. I find that it helps to remember how they grow naturally. Just as the most attractive way of planting daffodils and narcissus is in droves or large clumps, in order to form carpets of yellow and white, and not singly or in rows when the effect is stiff and unnatural, so the same principle applies when placing daffodils in vases. If they are used singly all facing forward the arrangement will be spiky and ugly. Instead pick up a handful of daffodils or narcissus – about five or six stems – and put them together into the container, allowing the stems to fall as they will. Remember that a daffodil is as pretty from the side as full face. Daffodils are very effective mixed with forsythia, in particular in a grey-stoned church.

Yellow flowers grow profusely in the summer, but they need to be planted carefully because the colour is a very powerful one and therefore liable to dominate everything in its neighbourhood. I love it beside cream and white or grey; but I hate it in direct contrast to red. The two colours together are very strident, but many flower arrangers will disagree with me. I have often seen the combination of red and yellow in churches, both at flower festivals and on other occasions. Be that as it may, to me the effect seems crude; yellow and orange, on the other hand, go very well together.

I know a very pretty small garden, which has an entirely deep to pale yellow, cream and white colour scheme, with lots of variegated and yellow-leaved shrubs and a collection of excellent grey plants. This colour scheme is equally good in summer flower arrangements. Grey foliage and white and cream flowers enhance pale and deep yellow. Green and pale grey walls make a particularly good background.

There are occasions when a solid yellow group makes a great impact; for example, in a dark-panelled room. In such a setting green foliage must be avoided, as it takes away from the brightness of the yellow. It is essential to have yellow-leaved plants and perhaps one or two variegated sprays. I do suggest that flower arrangers should strive to have an interesting collection of special material of this kind. I wonder whether other people scan garden catalogues as I do searching for 'aureo-' in the names of plants as an indication of golden or yellow foliage?

Very often shrubs with yellow leaves have little in the way of flowers, but are nonetheless well worth growing for their foliage. *Philadelphus coronarius* 'Aureus', for example, has good yellow leaves but tiny insignificant flowers. We have one planted in front of a grey *Eucalyptus gunnii* and a very dark mahonia, and it lends a splendid splash of colour. The foliage lasts reasonably well in water.

Throughout the summer and autumn the flower arranger's garden should provide plenty of yellow flowers for large mixed groups as well as small posies. The yellow 'Enchantment' lily grows easily and makes a good contribution to a mixed group; so does 'Connecticut King', a clear daffodil-yellow lily. Then there are yellow antirrhinums and roses and the cascading stems of genista (broom); 'Lydia' is a good yellow variety.

While oranges and reds are predominant colours in autumn, there are good yellow flowers too, such as dahlias, zinnias, and that jewel among rudbeckias, Black-eyed Susan (*Rudbeckia fulgida*). This splendid daisy-like flower has a dark brown cone-like centre which makes it unusual. It flourishes from midsummer through to autumn. I use it constantly for the house and church arrangements. The yellow stands out well against most dark backgrounds.

4 Ferns and ground cover
A: *Polystichum setiferum divisilobum densum*
B: Ivy
C: *Iris foetidissima* 'Variegata'
D: *Pulmonaria* foliage
E: *Lamium maculatum*

F: *Alchemilla mollis* foliage
G: *Asplenium*
H: *Astranta* foliage
I: *Ajuga*
J: *Dryopteris felix-mas cristata*
K: *Athyrium felix-femina*

Colour grouping

I have now discussed individual colours and the need when using them to take account of light and background. There are times, however, when the garden can only provide a mixed bunch. What looked lovely growing outside is sometimes disappointing when cut and arranged in a vase. If this is so the chances are that not enough care has been taken over the grouping and placing of different colours and types of plant material.

In a herbaceous border the eye is caught by sudden contrasts of colours, the success of which depends upon how the colour is used. The same principle applies when arranging flowers for the house, especially a large group which is to be seen from a distance. The object must always be to achieve a good overall shape. Get your outline, making sure that it is not too heavy, and then group your colours from that. If you have a few particularly striking flowers like lilies, they can best be used by keeping them together. Remember that the darker flowers will give emphasis and depth; so too will dark leaves, but they must be used carefully, otherwise they may spoil the general effect.

Once the general structure is in place flowers of different colours can be added as you please. Mixed bunches of sweet peas or garden pinks are best divided into different colours and shades massed together. If the container is a round one, get the colours to flow from one side across to the other. You will not achieve a good circular shape if you put all the bright colours on one side and the pale on the other as the effect will be unbalanced. If you are using only two colours separate the colours but let one flow gradually into the other. For example, if you are using blue and white, have the blue at the top and slightly to the right. Then bring it down through the middle to the left. Start the white similarly at the top, but slightly to the left, and bring it down across to the right. If colours are severely separated they end up looking like a regimental tie.

A mixed group is best placed against a plain background. The flowers will merge into a patterned wallpaper.

3. Tables of flowering seasons

In the tables which follow I have listed by colour

1. Shrubs
2. Climbers
3. Herbaceous plants – that is, plants that lose their leaves and stems at the end of the growing season
4. Bulbs, corms, tubers and rizomes

In each case I have shown the flowering season. The division between herbaceous plants and bulbs etc. (many of which are in fact herbaceous) is somewhat arbitrary, but it has seemed convenient to separate the more obvious bulbous plants.

In the tables I have shown only the botanical names; where popular names are in common use they will be found in the index.

In the case of both the shrubs and the climbers I have indicated those that are grown for their foliage rather than for their flowers (F), and for the shrubs I have also indicated those which have good berries (B) and are evergreen (E). In a few cases special features are shown after the name.

I have not included

1. Chrysanthemum 'Tricolor', clarkia, cosmos, helichrysum, pansy, polyanthus and Salvia horminum, which have a wide range of colours and a long flowering season
2. Grey plants, because they are all foliage plants, and are listed separately on page 59
3. Ground cover

Shrubs

(B) = berries
(E) = evergreen
(F) = foliage

	Spring	Summer	Autumn	Winter
Blue				
Caryopteris × clandonensis 'Arthur Simmonds'		*	*	
'Kew Blue'		*		
Ceratostigma willmottianum		*	*	
Hydrangea 'Blue Wave'		*		
Rosmarinus officinalis (E)	*	*		
Viburnum tinus 'Eve Price' (blue berries)			*	*
Green				
Fatsia japonica (E)	*	*	*	*
F. japonica 'Variegata' (E)	*	*	*	*
Garrya elliptica (E) (catkins)	*			*
Viburnum opulus 'Sterile'	*	*		
Mauve and purple				
Daphne mezereum				*
Erica carnea (E)	*			*
Orange				
Azalea kaempferi	*			
Potentilla 'Tangerine'		*	*	
Pyracantha lalandii (E)			*	
Pink				
Berberis thunbergii 'Nana' (F)			*	
Camellia 'Donation' (E)	*			*
C. elegans (E)	*			*
Chaenomeles speciosa 'Moerloesii'	*			
Deutzia 'Perle Rose'		*		
Erica	*			*
Escallonia 'Apple Blossom' (E)		*		
'Donard Brilliance' (E)		*		
'Edinensis' (E)		*		
'Slieve Donard' (E)		*		
Euonymus europaeus (B)			*	
Kolwitzia amabilis 'Pink Cloud'		*		
Pieris japonica 'Forest Flame' (E) (F)	*			
Prunus subhirtella 'Autumnalis Rosea'			*	*

Shrubs

(B) = berries
(E) = evergreen
(F) = foliage

	Spring	Summer	Autumn	Winter
Ribes sanguineum 'Tydeman's White'	*			
Rosa 'Cecile Brunner'		*	*	
'Queen Elizabeth'		*	*	
'Sweet Fairy'		*	*	
Sorbus vilmorinii (B)			*	
Symphoricarpus 'Mother of Pearl' (B)			*	
Viburnum × *bodnantense*	*			*
Weigela 'Abel Carriere'		*		

Red

	Spring	Summer	Autumn	Winter
Azalea kaempferi	*	*		
Camellia japonica 'Adolphe Audusson' (E)	*			*
Cornus alba 'Elegantissima' (red bark)	*	*	*	*
Cotoneaster hybridus pendulus (B)			*	
'John Waterer' (B)			*	
Erica carnea 'Eileen Pouter' (E)			*	
E. vivelli (E)			*	
Escallonia macrantha (E)		*		
Euonymus europaeus (B)			*	
Fuchsia 'Phyllis'		*		
Ribes sanguineum 'Pulborough Scarlet'	*			
Rosa rubrifolia (B) (F) (red hips)			*	
R. 'Tinkerbell'		*	*	
Skimmia japonica (B) (E)	*			
Weigela 'Bristol Ruby'		*		

Variegated

	Spring	Summer	Autumn	Winter
Acuba japonica 'Golden Spangles' (E) (F)	*	*	*	*
Arundinaria 'Variegata'	*	*	*	
A. 'Viridistriata'	*	*	*	
Buxus sempervirens 'Aureovariegata' (E)	*	*	*	*
'Elegantissima' (E)	*	*	*	*
Daphne odora 'Aureomarginata' (E)	*	*	*	*
Elaeagnus dicksonii (E)	*	*	*	*
Euonymus fortunei 'Emerald 'n' Gold' (E)	*	*	*	*
E. fortunei 'Silver Queen' (E)	*	*	*	*
Fatsia japonica 'Variegata' (E)	*	*	*	*

Shrubs

(B) = berries
(E) = evergreen
(F) = foliage

	Spring	Summer	Autumn	Winter
Fuchsia magellanica gracilis 'Variegata'		*	*	
Griselinia littoralis 'Variegata' (E)	*	*	*	*
Hebe 'Variegata' (E)	*	*	*	*
Ilex × altaclarensis 'Golden King' (E)	*	*	*	*
I. crenata 'Golden Gem' (E)	*	*	*	*
Pieris japonica 'Variegata'	*	*		
Pittosporum tenuifolium 'Garnetti' (E)	*	*	*	*
Ruta graveolens 'Variegata' (E)	*	*	*	*
Spiraea 'Anthony Waterer'		*	*	
Vinca major 'Elegantissima' (E)	*	*	*	*
Weigela 'Variegata' (F)		*	*	

White and cream

	Spring	Summer	Autumn	Winter
Azalea kaempferi	*			
Camellia 'Ama-no-kawa' (E)	*			*
Chaenomeles speciosa 'Nivalis'	*			
Choisya ternata (E)	*	*		
Cornus kousa chinensis		*		
Cytisus × praecox	*			
Daphne mezereum				*
Deutzia gracilis		*		
Eucryphia glutinosa		*	*	
E. 'Rostrevor' (E)		*	*	
Fatsia japonica			*	
Hydrangea 'Lanarth White'		*		
H. paniculata 'Grandiflora'		*		
Leycesteria formosa (B) (black berries)		*	*	
Magnolia stellata	*			
Philadelphus 'Belle Etoile'		*		
'Boule d'argent'		*		
'Manteau d'Hermine'		*		
Pieris japonica (E)	*			
Potentilla 'Veitchii'		*	*	
Prunus subhirtella 'Autumnalis'			*	*
Pyrus salicifolia 'Pendula'	*			
Rosa 'Pascale'		*		

Shrubs

(B) = berries
(E) = evergreen
(F) = foliage

	Spring	Summer	Autumn	Winter
Skimmia japonica (E)	*			
Spiraea × *arguta* (bridal wreath)	*			
Symphoricarpus 'White Hedge' (B)			*	
Syringa 'Madame Lemoine'	*			
Viburnum × *burkwoodii*	*			*
V. farreri				*
V. tinus (E)	*		*	*
Weigela 'Avalanche'		*		

Yellow

	Spring	Summer	Autumn	Winter
Arundinaria (F)	*	*	*	
Corylopsis spicata				*
C. willmottiae	*			
Corylus avellana 'Contorta' (catkins)	*			
Cotoneaster frigidus (B)			*	
Cytisus × *praecox*	*			
Elaeagnus pungens 'Aurea' (E) (F)	*	*	*	*
E. pungens 'Maculata' (E) (F)	*	*	*	*
Erica vulgaris sealei 'Aurea' (F)			*	
Forsythia suspensa atrocaulis	*			
Hamamelis mollis				*
Kerria japonica 'Pleniflora'	*			
Ligustrum 'Aureum' (E)	*	*	*	*
Philadelphus coronarius 'Aurea' (F)		*	*	
Potentilla fruticosa 'Katherine Dykes'		*		
Pyracantha 'Aurea' (E)			*	
'Flava' (E)			*	
Syringa 'Primrose'	*			

Climbers

(F) = foliage

	Spring	Summer	Autumn	Winter
Blue				
Clematis 'The President'		*		
Green				
Clematis cirrosa 'Balearica'	*			*
Cobaea scandens		*	*	
Fatshedera (F)	*	*	*	*
Mauve and purple				
Clematis 'Barbara Jackman'		*	*	
'Perle d'azure'		*		
Cobaea scandens		*	*	
Lathyrus latifolius		*	*	
Vitis vinifera 'Purpurea' (purple-leaved)		*	*	
Orange				
Rosa 'Schoolgirl'		*		
Tropaeolum		*	*	
Pink				
Clematis 'Lincoln Star'		*		
Rosa 'Compassion'		*		
'Ophelia'		*		
'Zepherine Drouhin'		*	*	
Red				
Tropaeolum speciosum		*	*	
White and cream				
Clematis 'Henri'		*		
'Marie Boisselot'		*		
Jasminum officinale		*		
Lonicera periclymenum 'Serotina'	*	*		
Rosa 'Iceberg'		*	*	
Yellow				
Clematis tangutica		*	*	
Hedera helix 'Buttercup' (F)	*	*	*	*
'Goldheart' (F)	*	*	*	*
Humulus lupulus aureus (F)		*	*	

Climbers

(F) = foliage

	Spring	Summer	Autumn	Winter
Jasminum nudiflorum				*
Lonicera 'aureoreticulata' (F)	*	*	*	
L. periclymenum 'Belgica'	*	*		
Rosa 'Golden Showers'		*		
Tropaeolum majus		*	*	
Vitis ampelopsis brevipedunculata (F)			*	

Herbaceous Plants

	Spring	Summer	Autumn	Winter
Blue				
Anchusa italica		*	*	
Aster 'King George'		*	*	
Brunnera macrophylla 'Variegata'	*			
Campanula		*		
Gentiana acaulis	*			
G. asclepiadea		*		
Geranium 'Buxton's variety'			*	
Myosotis (forget-me-not)	*			
Nigella		*		
Scabiosa caucasica 'Clive Greaves'		*	*	
Brown				
Coreopsis		*		
Crocosmia 'Emily McKenzie'		*	*	
Rudbeckia		*	*	
Green				
Alchemilla mollis	*	*		
Amaranthus caudatus 'Viridis'		*	*	
Angelica		*		
Echinops		*		
Helleborus corsicus	*			*
H. foetidus	*	*		

Herbaceous Plants

	Spring	Summer	Autumn	Winter
Heuchera sanguinea		*		
Moluccella laevis		*		
Nicotiana 'Limelight'		*	*	
Polygonatum multiflorum	*	*		
Zinnia 'Envy'		*	*	

Mauve and purple

	Spring	Summer	Autumn	Winter
Aquilegia		*		
Aster (Michaelmas daisy)		*	*	
Callistephus chinensis		*		
Campanula		*		
Cynara cardunculus		*	*	
Delphinium 'Black Knight'		*		
Erigeron		*		
Geranium 'Buxton's variety'			*	
Hosta		*		
Lunaria biennis	*			
Matthiola (stock)		*		
Nepeta		*	*	
Passiflora caerulea		*		
Penstemon 'Sour Grapes'		*	*	
Phlox 'Hampton Court'		*		
Pulsatilla vulgaris	*			
Pyrethrum		*		
Salvia horminum		*		
Scabiosa		*		
Thalictrum (F)		*		

Orange

	Spring	Summer	Autumn	Winter
Alstroemeria		*		
Antirrhinum		*		
Calendula		*	*	
Crocosmia 'Lucifer'		*	*	
Eremurus		*		
Papaver		*		
Physalis franchetii		*	*	
Zinnia		*	*	

Herbaceous Plants

	Spring	Summer	Autumn	Winter
Pink				
Alstroemeria		*		
Anemone japonica		*	*	
Antirrhinum		*		
Aquilegia		*		
Aster 'Elma Potschke'		*		
Clarkia		*		
Dianthus barbatus		*		
D. 'Doris'		*		
Dicentra spectabilis	*			
Delphinium 'Astolat'		*		
Digitalis		*		
Eremurus		*		
Erigeron		*		
Paeonia		*		
Papaver		*		
Penstemon 'Evelyn'		*	*	
Phlox		*		
Saxifraga umbrosa	*			
Sedum		*	*	
Verbascum		*		
Red				
Alstroemeria		*		
Antirrhinum		*		
Callistephus chinensis		*		
Dianthus barbatus		*		
Kniphofia		*		
Lobelia cardinalis		*		
Matthiola (stock)		*		
Nicotiana alata		*	*	
Paeonia		*		
Pentstemon 'Garnet'		*	*	
Pyrethrum		*		
White and cream				
Anemone japonica 'White Queen'		*	*	
Antirrhinum		*		
Aquilegia		*		

Herbaceous Plants

	Spring	Summer	Autumn	Winter
Astrantia		*		
Campanula		*		
Chrysanthemum frutescens		*		
C. maximum 'Mayfield Giant'		*		
C. maximum 'Silver Princess'		*		
C. spectabilis		*		
Clarkia		*		
Convallaria majalis	*			
Delphinium 'Galahad'		*		
Dianthus 'Hayter'		*		
Digitalis		*		
Gypsophila		*		
Helleborus niger				*
Iberis	*	*		
Matthiola		*		
Nicotiana		*	*	
Paeonia		*		
Pyrethrum 'Midsummer'		*		
Scabiosa caucasica 'Bressingham White'		*	*	

Yellow

	Spring	Summer	Autumn	Winter
Achillea		*		
Antirrhinum		*		
Dianthus		*		
Digitalis		*		
Doronicum	*			
Eremurus		*		
Rudbeckia		*	*	
Sisyrinchium		*		
Solidago		*	*	
Verbascum		*		
Zinnia		*		

Bulbs, corms, tubers and rhizomes

	Spring	Summer	Autumn	Winter
Blue				
Agapanthus 'Headbourne hybrids'		*		
Anemone 'De Caen'	*			
'St Brigid'	*			
Chionodoxa luciliae	*			
Endymion hispanicus 'Excelsior'	*			
Iris reticulata 'Harmony'	*			
Muscari	*			
Scilla bifolia	*			
Brown				
Iris 'Bearded'		*		
Lilium martagon		*		
Green				
Gladiolus 'Green Woodpecker'		*		
Tulipa 'Viridiflora Praecox'	*			
Mauve and purple				
Allium		*		
Colchicum			*	
Crocus	*			
Fritillaria meleagris	*			
Iris reticulata	*			*
I. unguicularis				*
Lilium martagon		*		
Orange				
Fritillaria imperialis	*			
Lilium 'Enchantment'		*		
Pink				
Cyclamen coum	*		*	
C. neapolitanum			*	
Endymion hispanicus 'Queen of the Pinks	*			
Gladiolus nanus 'Peach Blossom'		*		
G. 'Robinette'		*		
Hyacinthus cynthella	*			
Nerine bowdenii		*	*	
Schizostylis coccinea 'Mrs Hegarty'			*	
S. coccinea 'Viscountess Byng'			*	

Bulbs, corms, tubers and rhizomes

	Spring	Summer	Autumn	Winter
Red				
Anemone 'De Caen'	*			
'St Brigid'	*			
Dahlia 'Dazzler'		*	*	
Schizolstylis coccinea 'Major Scarlet'			*	
Variegated (grown for foliage)				
Iris foetidissima 'Variegata'	*	*	*	*
White and cream				
Colchicum speciosum 'Album'			*	
Cyclamen coum	*			*
C. neapolitanum		*	*	
Dahlia 'Easter Sunday'		*	*	
Endymion hispanicus 'Mount Everest'	*			
Galanthus	*			
Gladiolus nanus 'The Bride'		*	*	
Hyacinthus cynthella 'The Bride'	*			
Lilium auratum		*		
L. brownii		*		
L. candidum		*		
L. Enchantment 'Mont Blanc'		*		
Narcissus	*			
Tulipa 'White Triumphator'	*			
Zantedeschia 'Crowborough Variety'	*			
Yellow				
Crocus	*			
Dahlia 'Winter Dawn'		*	*	
'Yellowhammer'		*	*	
Erythronium tuolumnense	*			
Fritillaria imperialis	*			
Narcissus (including daffodil)	*			
Tulipa 'Page Poker'	*			

4. Conditioning

Conditioning is a word constantly used by flower arrangers because over the years we have come to recognize that flowers must be conditioned if they are to last in water. What the term means is the preparation of flowers and foliage well in advance of use so as to ensure that they will last as long as possible. I am, I know, considered by pupils from my flower classes to be a terrible 'conditioning' bore! Nevertheless, I stand my ground and say that it is pointless to grow lovely plant material and then allow it to wilt after picking, simply from neglect.

In this chapter I shall deal first with basic conditioning, that is to say, the treatment required by flowers and foliage generally. I shall then describe various forms of special treatment, appropriate in special cases.

Basic conditioning

The first matter to consider is the process of cutting. The best time for cutting is the evening or early morning. If for some reason cutting has to be done in sunlight, take a bucket with you into the garden and place the stems at once in water. Alternatively, I use a trug basket because the shape allows the stems to lie naturally. Do not overfill the trug; it is very easy to damage precious flowers.

It is very important to those of us who are keen gardeners as well as keen flower arrangers that we care for both our interests when cutting. In the days when my flower arranging seemed to be more important than my gardening the poor shrubs took a severe bashing! I was so keen to create a beautifully proportioned vase that I was prepared to hack away at the shrubs regardless of destroying their shape and sometimes even their chances of survival. It has to be faced that a small immature garden cannot supply all the plant material that you need as a flower arranger. New shrubs have to be allowed to establish themselves. The urge to snip just a twig or two has to be resisted. If the garden is big and mature enough there may be several specimens of the same shrub. In that case pick from each, not just one of them, and think in terms of the shape that you are leaving. Take from the left and the right, and cut any untidy pieces. If you require short pieces, cut back to the length required. Do make sure that you are not leaving ugly bare stems with no leaves or shoots to hide them. When foliage is scarce it is helpful to think in advance how many stems you require.

If the garden is very small there are unlikely to be many flowers or shrubs of the same type. When picking make sure that some stems with buds or other new growth are left. It is not worth stripping the garden for any arrangement. If it is to be a small summer posy with roses, take them from stems leaving buds for further blooms. I find Iceberg, for example, very suitable. Its buds are on long stems, so they can be picked individually for a little vase; and this applies to many flowering shrubs and plants. Exactly the same rule applies to leaves. I find that I have to be very firm over my *Arum italicum*. I am so excited when the leaves first appear that I have to resist the temptation to rush out and pick them before they have reached their full size and beauty, which would be very wasteful. In a small garden it is always foolish to overpick.

Having cut your material it is essential that it is given a long drink in a cool place, ideally for 24 hours. If you have a busy schedule, it is better to cut 48 hours in advance rather than to wait till the last minute so that the material is not left long enough in water. Most material likes to be put in deep warm water. There are one or two exceptions which are noted in the specialized lists at the end of this chapter. If flowers like gladioli, lilies, irises, paeonies, etc., are needed for a special occasion, they may well need to be picked a week ahead to allow them to open naturally. If, on the other hand, flowers are coming out too quickly, for instance roses or tulips, wrap several stems together in newspaper and plunge them into iced water. This will stop them from coming out too soon. All leaves below the water level should be removed.

All shrubs need to have their stems hammered. Place them on a hard surface and hammer about one inch from the bottom of the stem, so that it is well split. This ensures that the water will reach to the top of the stems. Remove the lower leaves and plunge the stems into warm water.

The stems of flowers should be cut about one inch up before they are given their preliminary drink. Stems can harden in a very short time. If there is time, each stem should be re-cut before being arranged in a vase.

When you have completed your flower arrangement, fill the container as near to the top as you dare! In about two hours' time, re-fill. It is in the first two hours that flowers drink the most. The vase should be topped up every morning or evening. If the vase is on a polished table, put a tea towel round the base when you top up as a protection, as sometimes the flowers syphon with disastrous results. Alas! at least three of my tables bear witness to overflowing containers. If possible, place the container on a glass mat.

Arrangements should also be sprayed. Most garden centres and shops sell a fine spray. Both flowers and foliage should be watered with a spray as soon as the arrangement is complete, especially in hot weather. If the vase is against a valuable wallpaper or panelling, do protect the background. I get someone to hold up a tea towel while I spray.

Special treatment

Boiling water

This is to me a miraculous treatment which I use more and more. It sounds quite extraordinary, but it works! Put the stems into a bucket and pour in boiling water to a depth of about an inch. Leave the stems for about one minute and then fill up the bucket with cold water. I list at the end of this chapter the material that needs this treatment – among them poppies, delphiniums, euphorbia and vinca.

Boiling water and sugar

This special treatment is the same as that described above, except that about two tablespoons of granulated sugar are added. It is particularly good for roses.

Sugar

Sugar puts back a substance which tulips need. Dissolve two tablespoons of sugar in water and put the tulips into it. If the flowers droop when arranged in a vase, take them out, cut the stems, and give them a further drink of the sugar solution.

Searing

This is an alternative to the boiling water method and provides a quick way of sealing the ends of flowers. Euphorbia, for instance, bleeds off a sticky substance and searing will prevent this bleeding. Simply hold the stems over a flame.

Starch

Some leaves and ferns need strengthening. This can be effected by two teaspoons of starch to one and a half pints of water. This process of stiffening will make the material easier to arrange.

Floating

Many leaves, like those of hostas, arums and ferns, last far longer if they are floated in a basin or bath. I leave them for several hours and then use them in the ordinary way. Remember if you are arranging them in a vase on a polished table that they may drip, with disastrous consequences! If there is any risk, protect the table until they have dried off.

Filling hollow stems with water

This is an alternative to the boiling water treatment and I think it is better for very tall delphiniums. Simply turn the flower upside down, fill the stem with water, plug the end with cotton wool, and then place in a vase in the ordinary way. You must first decide what height you want the flower to be, as obviously the stem cannot be cut once it has been filled!

Pricking stems
The stems of some flowers form bubbles that prevent water from reaching up to the flower heads. Tulips and hellebores are particularly prone to doing this. To prevent this take the stem and pierce it just below the head very carefully with a needle, continuing the process down the stem at intervals of about two inches. This will ensure that water reaches the top of the stem.

Retaining roots
Some flowers, for example poinsettias, bleed when cut and therefore do not last well in water. If, however, they are dug up roots and all and carefully placed in a polythene bag tied at the top of the root, they can be used in flower decorating. This is a good way of using many plants, such as *Begonia rex*, chlorophytum and ivies, mixed with cut flowers. When the flowers are dead the plants can be put back into the garden. If the plants are needed at a height, they can be lashed on to sticks.

Boiling vinegar
This is excellent for bamboos. Pour boiling vinegar into a jug to the depth of about one inch. Strip off the bark from the end of the stems and insert them into the vinegar for five minutes. Then give them a long drink.

Polythene bag treatment
Some plant material and leaves are best transported in a large, sealed polythene bag. I sometimes put a tiny bit of water inside to keep it moist.

Disasters
If several flowers in an arrangement droop, take them out. In most cases the boiling water treatment will revive them. Put them into a bucket and give them a further long drink. Then put them back into the arrangement. If roses or tulips wilt, give them the boiling water and sugar treatment and a long drink. If hellebores wilt, take them out and re-float them for an hour or so. I find that many hellebores, such as orientalis, are better arranged in deep water.

5. Dried material

Before I became interested in gardening the flower arranger within me always won. If I saw flowers in the garden which I particularly wanted for the house I would cut ruthlessly, regardless of the poor denuded beds. Nowadays the battle between garden and house is more evenly fought.

A great joy of drying and preserving plant material is that one can have the best of both worlds. The plant as it grows gives pleasure in the garden. Then as it fades, the petals fall and marvellous seed heads appear. It is ripe for drying and provides further enjoyment in the house. Of course, dried material is by no means confined to seed heads. There is a very wide range of plants that are easily preserved. In some cases the plant as it fades dries quite naturally and only needs to be cut and carefully stored.

A successful dried arrangement must include different textures, shapes and colours. Gone are the days of rather depressing vases filled with bullrushes, pampas grass and a few, sad Chinese lanterns.

One should aim to build up an interesting collection, remembering that experiment is the keynote of preservation. Watch what your friends preserve and find out their methods. Then if your own garden has strikingly coloured leaves, interesting plants or berries, explore how best to keep them. Remember, too, that small posies can be just as useful as large formal groups. If you have a few fresh leaves and flowers which need augmenting, add dried material. If it has to go into water or Oasis, either seal the ends of the stalks with sealing wax or wind small pieces of tin foil round them. The chestnut roaster illustrated on colour pl. 8 has dried seed heads among the foliage, all pushed into Oasis.

There are many excellent specialized books on the drying and preservation of plant material, so in this chapter I discuss only the simpler methods, which are nevertheless perfectly adequate for most purposes.

When to pick

If the plant material is to be successfully preserved it must be in very good condition when picked, so keep an eagle eye on your garden and preferably pick on a dry day. Early morning dew on the plants is not a good idea. Should it be necessary to pick in damp conditions, shake the plant well and lay it out on a sheet of blotting paper as the first step; alternatively gently remove the moisture from the leaves with a dry tissue.

Certain flowers need to be carefully watched so that they are picked at the right moment. Everlasting flowers like aeroclinium, rhodanthe and helichrysum must be picked as they are opening. Larkspur and delphinium need to be picked when the flower is fully out. Hydrangea should be picked as the flower head is just starting to dry off at the edges; very immature heads will simply flop.

Most seed heads will dry naturally on the plant provided that there has been a spell of warm weather. If there is any likelihood of rain, however, it is better to pick the head and to dry it artificially.

Drying

The ideal place to dry material is a darkish room with a good circulation of air and a continually dry atmosphere. The drying process should be as quick as possible. Garages and sheds can be a snare and delusion because they are often slightly damp.

I am fortunate in having a landing with an open banister running the whole length from which I hang-dry material (see fig. 5). The advantage of this position is that there is a radiator in the hall below which sends up warm air and another on the landing itself, so material dries very quickly. I am able to have a continuous stream of small special treasures under my eye.

Many people are fortunate enough to have a large airing cupboard, which is excellent for tall flowers like delphiniums, which need special warmth. All leaves should be removed from the stems and if necessary dried separately. Leaves left on a stem increase the moisture level and simply shrivel.

Hang-drying
This term is used for the method of drying whereby a small bunch of stems or seed heads tied together is hung upside down to dry (see fig. 5). It is fatal to have too many stems bunched together – about five is the maximum – and the heads should not be allowed to touch. If I have something very special I dry each stem individually. I use garden twine or raffia tied with a slip knot because stems shrink as they dry and to prevent them from slipping down the twine may need to be tightened.

There are hundreds of plants which can be dried by this method. I have found it very successful in the case of the following:

Acanthus: flower heads
Alchemilla mollis: flower heads when fully open

5 Bunches of flower and seed heads hanging upside down to dry

Allium

Amaranthus caudatus: (love-lies-bleeding): remove leaves

Aquilegia: when the seed heads are fully open

Clarkia: flowers dry well

Clematis tangutica: the fluffy seed heads

Delphinium: when seed heads come open

Digitalis (foxglove): when the seed heads are fully open

Echinops ritro: cut the stems as the blue flower heads begin to open

Erica 'heather': pick when the flowers are just open

Gypsophila: when flowers are fully open

Helichrysum (straw daisy): pick when fully open and bind a wire on to the stems
    before drying as they are very brittle

Humulus (hop)

Helipterum: this has very pretty pink and white everlasting flowers which retain
    their colour when dried

Lavatera (the seed heads)

Lavandula

Lunaria biennis (honesty): dry before the outside seed pod has got damp so that
    it will not mark the pretty translucent membrane. Once it is quite dry shake
    or peel off the pods and stand in a jug

Lupinus: the very good seed heads dry well

Nigella (love-in-the-mist): this has one of the most beautiful seed heads, varying in colour from cream to purple. Remove most of the frondy leaves, save for a few near the seed head

Papaver (poppy): every sort has lovely blue-green seed heads. Shake out the seeds first for next year's sowing

Physalis (Chinese lantern): dry the orange seed heads having first removed all the leaves

Sedum: when flowers are fully open

Senecio: the leaves, silver on one side and green on the other, dry well

Sisyrinchium: the seed heads go a wonderful brown (see colour pl. 8)

Stachys lanata: all seed heads dry well

Glycerine

The disadvantage of hang-drying is that material treated in this way becomes brittle and leaves are easily split. The alternative is to use a solution of glycerine or anti-freeze. The advantage of preserving foliage and berries in this way is that they remain pliable with a good shiny surface and are easy to handle. The only snag is that leaves become darker, some changing from green to dark brown. The problem can be slightly countered by placing the newly treated material in a well lighted area, preferably in front of a window, where it will not change colour so much.

To make the solution mix one part of glycerine with two pints of very hot water in a container with a lid – large coffee jars are excellent for this purpose – and shake it well to ensure complete mixing. While the mixture must always be warm when made, for very hard wooded stems it must be brought to boiling point. Then, of course, a glass container cannot be used as it would break. A mixture containing anti-freeze can be made in exactly the same way, save that the proportions of anti-freeze and water must be equal. Glycerine is more expensive than anti-freeze, but I find it more satisfactory. If any of the solution is left over it can be put into an air-tight jar and be heated and used on other occasions.

When selecting branches for preservation by this method be sure to look for pretty shapes, with some branches bending to the right and some to the left. They must at all events be in peak condition. Remove all leaves from the lower part of each stem, slit the ends, and if necessary scrape away some of the bark to allow the solution to get to the top of the branch. It is tempting to try to preserve leaves which have already changed colour, but you will not succeed because by that time the leaves are too mature.

Having prepared the branches, put the ends into the hot solution immediately. The solution should come about three inches up the stem, so use a narrow container if possible. Watch the material daily, as some plants drink more quickly than others. If all the solution is absorbed before the whole plant or branch is preserved, top up the container with more hot mixture, not boiling, to the original three-inch level.

Sometimes moisture beads appear on leaves, indicating that they have been in the solution too long. Take the material out and wipe off the beads with a tissue.

Occasionally very thick-tissued leaves like those of *Fatsia japonica* are unable to absorb enough of the liquid and become brittle at the edges. Leaves of this sort are best preserved by immersing them completely in a warm solution.

When they have changed colour and show no sign of brittleness you can assume that preservation is complete. Then take them out of the solution and place them on blotting paper until they are quite dry. After the preservation of berries is complete it is a good idea to spray them with a cheap lacquer hair-spray.

The time taken by the process of preservation varies. Laurel and other hard-wooded plants may take several weeks. In some cases the process may take only a few days. When preservation is complete the material can be used with fresh foliage and flowers as it will take up no more water.

Most foliage and some plants will respond to this treatment and it is worth while experimenting, using a few branches or leaves to begin with and adding to them if they react favourably. I have found most useful among the garden material which responds: *Fatsia japonica*, berberis, escalonia, *Helleborus corsicus*, paeony foliage, rowan (mountain ash), viburnum and single leaves of acer. Perhaps for the flower arranger mollucella (bells of Ireland) gives the most spectacular result. It should be treated as described above, but then hung upside down to dry. The bracts become papery and go a wonderful buff colour.

Under carpet method

To preserve single prettily coloured leaves and small ferns I place them between several layers of newspaper and put them under the drawing-room carpet. The room is kept reasonably warm and they are usually quite dry within about ten days, sometimes sooner. I then bind them onto twigs or stub wires with silver fuse wire and cover the twigs or wire with *gutta percha* or thin strips of green crepe paper.

Dried ferns or leaves in autumn colouring – acer is particularly good – make a winter posy of dried or fresh flowers more interesting.

Drying in water

The best way of drying some flowers is to put them into about two inches of water and allow them to dry off naturally. This is the ideal way for hydrangeas. Pick them when the flowers are just starting to become crisp at the edges. Stand them in a jug or bucket containing about three inches of water, having first removed the leaves. Allow them to dry off in their own time and do not at any time add water. Heathers and lavender also dry well in this way.

Upright drying

When hanging space is difficult to find; some material can be dried simply by being placed in a container in a dry room and left to dry off naturally. The following respond well to this method:

Achillea

Artichoke (globe): pick when the flowers are only half developed. Strip off all leaves and stand in a deep container to dry

Dianthi (pinks): pick when fully open and stand in a dark place until fully dry

Dianthus barbatus (sweet William): pick before the flower heads are fully open. When dry they retain charming pale, muted colours

Santolina: pick with the yellow flower heads, which will dry yellowish-brown

Ironing

This is a good method if dried leaves are needed quickly. Place the leaves between sheets of blotting paper or newspaper and press them with a warm iron. Spiky leaves like those of crocosmia and Iris *pseudacorus variegatus* are particularly well suited to this process.

Drying in desiccants such as borax

I find the methods which I have described above the easiest and most practical for the busy gardener and flower arranger. The more ambitious will find that a wide range of flowers can be dried in desiccants such as silica-gel, sand and borax. Of these borax is the simplest and the only desiccant that I use. I suggest that readers who wish to experiment in a more ambitious way buy a book specializing in dried material.

Household borax can be purchased from chemists' shops and household stores. It comes in 1 lb (or 500 g) packs and is cheaper than medicinal borax.

The principle in using desiccants is entirely to immerse the flower in the substance used so that not a petal or stamen is visible. I find that polythene sandwich boxes make very good containers. I put a layer of borax in the bottom of the box and place the flower on it. I then cover the flower with borax, shake the box gently, and if necessary cover the flower again. As borax is a light substance, use a small, soft paint brush to press it into all the cavities of the flower very carefully.

When you are quite certain that every crevice and cavity of the flower is filled, add a third layer of borax. Put the airtight lid firmly on and to make sure, seal the edges with sellotape. Stand it in a dry, warm room. The length of time needed for drying will depend upon the size and shape of the flower. After two days remove the sellotape, open the container and carefully remove the flower. Shake off the desiccant. If the flower is ready it will be crispy dry, almost like paper. If you are unsure, put it back, cover it as before and after another day or so test again. Once flowers are dry they should be stored in a warm, dry place away from the light. I stand them individually in a dry block of Oasis, upright and not touching one another.

Ornamental gourds

These are in a category of their own. Gourds can easily be grown from seed, provided that they are planted in a sunny position. The plant will grow along the ground like a vegetable marrow, or it can be trained up a trellis or wall. In the autumn the flowers will turn into large fruits of different shapes. Some orange fruits are as big as large cooking apples. There are very attractive dark green, striped fruits shaped like tangerines, and equally decorative creamy-white, oval ones.

They need to be picked when they are fully grown and in perfect condition. They must be stored in a very dry place. Some people varnish them with a colourless varnish, which helps to preserve them, but they are prettier if left in their natural state. If a fruit starts to decay it must be removed at once or it will affect the rest.

Storage

I have referred above to some special methods of storage: for example, in the case of flowers preserved with desiccants. Generally, dried material can be kept standing in buckets or vases in a cool, dry place, and I find that it can be stored successfully in dress boxes between layers of tissue paper. Kept in this way it will last for several years. It is much better to dismantle an arrangement at the end of winter and store whatever is in good condition than to have it standing year after year gathering dust and losing all colour and shape.

Arranging

Dried material can be used in a variety of ways, from important groups in large houses to a tiny posy on a writing desk. Elsewhere I describe its use for garlands (see page 106) and ornamental trees (see page 119).

At the risk of treading on dangerous ground I must nevertheless say that I am getting a little bored by the sight of huge dark arrangements standing in halls month after month and becoming a decrepit part of the furniture. Likewise, large baskets stuffed with everlastings and frills of statice are – dare I say it? – becoming overdone. I prefer dried material used in conjunction with fresh flowers or as an arrangement which will be changed, not every week like fresh flowers, but several times during the winter months.

The general tendency with large groups is to arrange them against a wall with no light behind. In fact the most successful arrangements are those which have light coming through them so that there are several dimensions rather than a solid mass. The careful preserver will have collected material of different shapes and textures. Tall, pointed seed heads, like stems of delphinium or larkspur, give a good outline, but need to be used with rounded shapes like hydrangea heads and to be contrasted with the fluffy heads of alchemilla and gypsophila combined with good textured leaves preserved in glycerine – like fatsia, ivies, beech and so on. A good garden should supply a quantity of interesting shapes. For tiny posies everlasting flowers and gypsophila mixed with dried leaves and ferns are enchanting.

6. Mechanics

One of the first essentials when arranging flowers is to consider the best way of anchoring the plant material securely in its container, whether it is a tiny posy or a large pedestal arrangement. The method of doing this is described by flower arrangers as 'mechanics', a term that includes all the different aids available: the most popular are chicken wire, Oasis and pin-holders. I firmly believe that the simplest aids are the most effective.

Most flowers and foliage can be held in place perfectly successfully by using several layers of two inch mesh **chicken wire**, inserted into the container. The wire must be sufficiently firm so that stems can be pushed in at any angle and be held in place.

The easiest method is to cut a piece of chicken wire roughly to the size which appears to fit the container in question, remembering that a large one will need at least three and possibly as many as five layers of wire (see fig. 6). Fold the wire so that it is crumpled up into a ball of several layers and gently push it right down to the bottom of the container, taking care not to make the ball too tight or you will have difficulty in inserting the flowers. The top of the ball should overlap the edge of the container, forming a mushroom shape (see fig. 7). If there is insufficient wire the whole arrangement can easily topple out, causing terrible damage to polished surfaces. The expert will arrange a large vase of flowers in a good chicken wire base and carry it from room to room without a stem moving, thereby proving the value of good mechanics. A vase which has handles on either side is very desirable because the wire can be firmly tied to them.

Oasis is a splendid substance that holds water and is often invaluable for shallow containers which will not take much water and for making garlands (see page 109). Oasis comes in two shapes, brick-sized oblongs and small round segments. It is sold dry and must be soaked before use. I have discovered that the easiest way to prepare it is to put it in a basin or bucket of water and leave it to soak thoroughly. Whatever the manufacturers say, I always give it at least half an hour. What many people do, quite wrongly, is to jam several bricks together to soak them. I have even seen a weight used to hold them down. In

6 Filling a container with chicken wire

7 The correct placement of the chicken wire

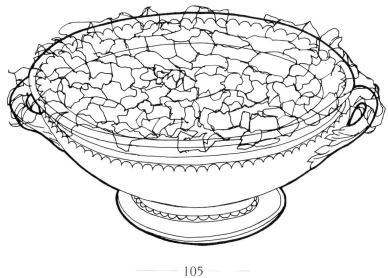

fact they should be allowed to float quite separately so as to soak up the water naturally. Then they can be cut with a knife to the required size. Make sure that the entire piece is dark green: a light area indicates that it is not wholly wet, and must be refloated.

Remember when using Oasis that it dries out very quickly, so that it must either be used in a container that will hold some water and be topped up regularly, or it must be encased in a plastic bag, as, for example, when used with the chestnut roaster shown on colour pl. 8. It is quite easy to pierce the bag, either with the stems of the material being used or with a knitting needle. The bag will preserve some moisture even though pierced, but the Oasis will eventually dry out.

Another use for Oasis is in silver and copper containers, which can easily be scratched by chicken wire.

The **pin-holder** is a useful accessory. It comes in various sizes and shapes, but always consists of a heavy circular metal base from which numerous spikes protrude upwards. The pin-holder sits at the bottom of the container and provides an anchor for heavy branches and stems. I use it in conjunction with chicken wire. It is also useful when a branch or two of a flowering shrub is arranged in a flat dish which cannot be wired because it is too shallow.

To enable short flowers to be brought up to a height there are very useful **plastic cones** of various sizes which are found in most good florists. The cones are pushed down into the chicken wire so that the plant material is extended by the length of the cones. If further height is required, lash the cones on to sticks and push the sticks into the wire. I do suggest that only fairly long-stemmed flowers are used with cones: six-foot high primroses are not a good idea!

There are now excellent **candle-cups** for use with candlesticks. They are simply little metal cups which hold water and fit into the tops of candlesticks as shown in fig. 8. The plant material is inserted into Oasis cut to fit inside the cups (see fig. 9). Fig. 10 shows a completed arrangement. In colour pl. 12 the red flowers have been arranged in this way.

Garlands

Garlands have many uses as decorations for special occasions. I have made them looped up at intervals with small bows for staircases and along the front of buffet tables and choir stalls. In churches I have also used them to frame the door in the porch and hanging from the tops of or twirling up pillars. Similarly, in marquees I have twined them up the poles.

A garland needs far more material than might be supposed. It should include a good foundation of greenery like box or cupressus – the latter used very sparingly, as it can easily become too heavy – and small sprays of berried ivy, together with pieces of coloured foliage like euonymus and privet. The fluffy

8 A candlestick filled with a candle-cup

9 The initial placement of flowers in the Oasis inside the candlestick

limey-green heads of alchemilla are very effective, as is cow parsley, provided in its case that it is well conditioned by the boiling water method. A very attractive garland can, indeed, be made without using flowers at all, provided that contrasting leaves are used at regular intervals. It will, however, look unbalanced if, for example, yellow leaves are dotted about irregularly without any kind of pattern.

If flowers are included, they should be carefully placed so that one colour shades into another, or else contrasting colours are used at regular intervals.

11 A 'string of sausages'

12 Inserting sprays of flowers and foliage

If the garland curves (see fig. 13) it may be thought preferable to keep deep tones in the centre with the colours gradually fading as they reach the bows.

Garland mechanics

In the old days we used to machine long strips of polythene together to make a tube. Nowadays, I am thankful to say, it is possible to buy packs of ready-made polythene tubing of differing lengths and widths. I find that the three inch width is the most practical.

Measure the pillar or other place where the garland is to be and if it is to be looped allow enough extra footage, plus another foot at the end, when preparing the tube. Having cut the tube to the right length, tie one end with string, take a piece of Oasis about three inches in length and cut to such a size that it will fit snugly into the tube, and push it down to the tied end. Pinch the tube together immediately above the Oasis with a tie (of the kind sold with plastic bags). Continue the process until the tube is filled, and the other end tied as before, when it will look something like a long string of sausages (see fig. 11).

Lay the 'string of sausages' on a trestle table and push in small sprays of foliage and flowers (see fig. 12). It may be difficult to insert fragile stems, in which case make holes through the plastic with a knitting needle, and push the stems into the holes.

When the garland is complete tie it on to a hook or nail in a place where it can drip. The holes in the 'sausages' will for a time let out water and the drips could be disastrous on carpets or polished floors. When the garland has ceased to drip arrange it where it is required (see fig. 13). If it is to be used round the top of a pillar in a church, you will find that two people are needed, one to hold the garland up in the middle and the other to tie the two ends together.

Garlands of dried material
These can be made in the same way as garlands of fresh material except that dry Oasis is used.

Containers

To enjoy arranging flowers, particularly for special occasions, it is important to have an interesting and practical collection of containers. Nothing is more frustrating than to pick lovely flowers and find that you have nothing suitable in which to put them.

There are many suitable containers to be purchased, from beautiful china urns to simple plastic bowls. Vases should have good wide tops and be well proportioned. Too small a base may result in the vase overturning. Choose containers which will blend well with the background of your rooms. Very dominant, bright colours often lead the eye away from the flowers.

It is quite unnecessary to use only conventional vases. In spite of eager, hawk-eyed flower arrangers the junk shops still produce much of interest. Soup tureens can often be found and, if the lids are missing, are quite cheap. Gravy boats, jugs of every description and old-fashioned wash-basins are splendid for pedestals. Silver sugar bowls are good – the list goes on for ever! The important thing is to open your eyes and search for interesting shapes, textures – anything which will spark off an idea. I found in France a wonderful range of white fireproof dishes which have never seen the inside of my oven because they are the perfect shape for flowers.

When the container is secondary to the flowers, because they flow forwards and sideways so as to hide it, all that is needed is something deep enough to hold water and wide enough to let the contents flow naturally over the rim. Any large watertight bowl will suffice. There are, however, many occasions when a pretty vase is an important adjunct to the flowers. I have a rather charming white swan with a pale green and blue base and sufficient space for a large piece of Oasis to sit in. He makes a charming background for small spiky flowers.

There are many good market stalls and shops which sell a wide variety of baskets, some with their own containers. Natural cane or rush makes a perfect background for many simple garden flowers like daisies, cornflowers, polyanthus and daffodils. Baskets come in many shapes and sizes. There are tiny little ones which, if lined with tin-foil and filled with Oasis, are delightful for small alpines. There are much larger ones which will take small plants (see colour pl. 3). There are many with attractive handles which add a different dimension to the flowers. If the basket has not got its own container it can be made to hold moisture by means of Oasis in a plastic bag and set on tinfoil or the insertion of any bowl which will fit into it.

Whenever I see an interesting basket I buy it, not necessarily to keep it for myself but because flowers arranged in a basket make an attractive present, particularly for a sick friend, whether at home or in hospital.

7. Flowers for special occasions

When I talk of flowers for special occasions I mean party flowers. The occasion may be a small dinner party, for example, or a dance; but whatever form the party takes flowers should play an important role, providing as they do a sense of welcome. They do, moreover, provide essential colour to what might otherwise be a dull background if the party takes place in a public hall or a marquee.

While I shall discuss party flowers in some detail, a useful general rule is that it is usually better to restrict flowers to one or two important groups than to have a great many small posies. Furthermore, the colouring should echo some part of the surroundings for which it is planned. The general effect is improved if the flowers reflect curtains or cushions or even a striking picture. For instance, apricot curtains could be matched by flowers of the same shade fading off into cream and white. A deep pink or red wall might be a good background for such a clashing red group as discussed on page 72; but in this book I am, of course, only concerned with the flowers which you can grow in your own garden, and it may be difficult to achieve such an effect from the available material. At certain times of the year one can only expect to find a mixture of colouring in a small garden. Whereas mixed flowers can be very pretty, they need to be placed against a plain wall rather than a patterned paper.

There should be flowers to greet the guests the moment they enter the building. In a house with a large entrance hall a pedestal arrangement is instantly visible and safely out of harm's way. Guests always seem to arrive together, busily chatting and discarding coats and gloves, so small vases are unnoticed or even get swept away. Nothing is more dampening to the start of a party than flowers hurled to the floor in a crash of broken china, as I know to my cost!

Some houses are fortunate enough to have sweeping staircases leading up to a landing. For a special occasion like a wedding or dance I have either made garlands of dried flowers (see page 110) or in the summer filled them with *Alchemilla mollis* or cow parsley and looped them on to the banisters at intervals with ribbon bows. The effect is pretty and inexpensive!

14 The brass chestnut roaster

15 The chestnut roaster showing the initial placement of flowers

Sometimes in a hall one finds a large chest, which is convenient for an important group. Where the hall is too small for a big vase a hanging arrangement may be used. For instance, I have a brass chestnut roaster which hangs on a hook flat against the wall and looks very nice filled with flowers and foliage stuck into Oasis (see figs 14 and 15). At Christmas I fill it with variegated holly and attach bows of red ribbon. The mock orange trees which are shown on either side of a wedding cake in fig. 18 also look very pretty if placed on either side of a hall door as a special form of welcome.

The next room to consider when preparing for a party is the drawing-room. Obviously this will vary enormously in character from one house to another. We live in an old cottage with low ceilings which make pedestal arrangements impracticable. I like to have flowers above the heads of the guests so I use the top of a china cabinet as a base. A soup tureen fits there neatly. I back it with tall flowers and then have trailing material like honeysuckle, variegated vinca and ivy cascading over the edge.

A small round pedestal table makes a good place for a basket filled with little plants like polyanthus and miniature ivies which will afterwards go back into the garden (see colour pl. 2). If the party is a large one I will have one other important vase on a side table.

In a tall and formal drawing-room pedestal groups are ideal and large jugs are excellent containers for flowering shrubs and mixed arrangements. I have a very attractive jug by Michael Leach which is a great inspiration on many occasions. Jugs of all shapes and sizes are worth collecting. A tall looking-glass in a drawing-room makes an excellent background for flowers, particularly flowering shrubs, which reflect well.

Dinner parties

The dining-room is obviously the focal point of a dinner party. The size of the dining table and the number of guests will determine the amount of spaces available for flowers. While a large table makes an obvious setting for special decoration, I have known occasions when the hostess has allowed them to get quite out of hand. The guests have been confronted by huge bowls of tall flowers, making conversation with their opposite numbers quite impossible! If the conversation is to be general, the table decorations must be low!

Flowers in a dining-room should either be a part of the general background colour like the red ones in colour pl. 12, or provide a stunning contrast; for instance, apricot flowers arranged against a green wall, or mixed greens or yellows set against a grey or white background. As a change from a highly polished table a brightly-coloured cloth can be part of the general colour scheme making a brilliant contrast to flowers.

My rule in this book is to discuss only flowers which one can grow in the garden, but I am going to cheat a bit and include fruit and vegetables! When flowers are in short supply a superb central table decoration can be provided by means of fruit or ornamental gourds piled up in a dish. I sometimes tuck in a bit of coloured foliage at each end. In summer I sometimes have a bowl filled only with green grapes and peppers, and candlesticks arranged with variegated and green foliage. In our red dining-room the effect is cool and attractive.

When space is limited candlestick arrangements are very useful. The mechanics are discussed in detail on page 106. The great advantage of candlesticks is that they take up much less space on the table than ordinary flower arrangements and make elegant containers for honeysuckle, ivies and spray carnations. I have used them filled only with cow parsley and, later in the summer, daisies and snippets of grey foliage.

For winter dinner parties where space is limited I have made small trees of dried flowers; the method used is exactly the same as in the case of the large ones discussed on pages 117-19. The small daisy-like everlasting xeranthemum is ideal for this purpose. Nowadays there are baskets of every shape and size which are excellent for dried flowers. For one special party each lady guest had a tiny basket in front of her place and this was a great success!

Kitchen parties and buffet tables

Nowadays when we all seem to be so busy, entertaining in the kitchen has become part of the modern way of life. Our original kitchen was small and unattractive, but some years ago we moved it to the other end of the house. At the same time the kitchen was extended, so that now we have a cosy and warm place for informal entertaining. The eating area is enclosed on three sides by light pine panelling. The remainder of the walls are tiled in cream interspersed with Victorian tiles collected over many years. The brown and cream colours produce an effect of warmth, and brightness is provided by vivid pink and red window blinds.

I have a collection of coloured linen cloths – red, pink and orange – which make a splendid base for flowers and fruit and tie in with the background colours of the room. As appropriate to the informality of kitchen entertaining I use simple, pretty flowers, bowls filled with marigolds, daisies or small zinnias, rather than more formal flowers. During December, I have a small copper lustre jug sitting on the kitchen table filled with the last of the border carnations, two iceberg roses, a few stems of mauve and white campanula and pink nerines. The last of the summer flowers are very special, so I like to keep them in the kitchen under my eye.

There are occasions when food is laid out in the kitchen for a buffet supper party. Many years ago I was asked to arrange the flowers for a young people's party which was to start off in a large old-fashioned kitchen with a wonderful collection of copper pans hanging on the walls. We made a tablecloth of hessian and we plaited raffia to make garlands which were looped along the front of the table. Brightly coloured everlasting flowers, herbs and lavender were tied in bunches and held in place by large raffia bows pinned on to the front of the cloth. The central decoration was a large copper bowl filled with ornamental gourds and apples built up into a tall pyramid. Copper saucepans were placed at each end and filled with orange crocosmia, sprays of pyracanthus covered in orange berries, a mixture of pale apricot to deep orange dahlias and mixed yellow and orange rudbeckias and zinnias. The general effect was set off by vivid variegated foliage, some of it tucked into the central pyramid. Tall brass candlesticks held candle cups bearing orange candles and cascades of variegated ivy and physalis (cape gooseberry).

There were small tables spread between the kitchen and the dining-room which had blue and white check tablecloths. In the middle of each table was a small bowl filled with Oasis, in the centre of which was a blue candle, forming a central point round which were massed marigolds and ivy leaves. The whole area was lit only by the candles and it proved to be a very glowing sight.

There are other occasions when a buffet table is arranged in a more formal setting. White or pale-coloured tablecloths make a good foundation for decorations. Ivy looks pretty looped across the front of the table tied with ribbon bows. If it is a winter party dried flower garlands (see fig. 13) make a very pretty decoration, again looped and held by ribbon.

A buffet table needs a tall decoration in the centre and if it is a long table at either end as well. In this way the guests' attention is held the moment they enter the room. Most people will remember those old-fashioned saucepan stands shaped rather like a wigwam! There are usually about four shelves tapering off to a small one at the top. One of these stands makes an excellent foundation for a buffet table arrangement. I use round blocks of Oasis soaked and cut to fit saucers which sit on the shelves so as to form the base of a tall pyramid-shaped decoration. Flowers are heaped on to each shelf with lots of trailing ivy and sprays of flowering shrubs flowing over the edges and sides to hide the white plastic structure of the stand. If preferred, however, this can be painted gold or silver, in which case it need not be entirely covered. The gold or silver is quite pretty appearing through the flowers and foliage.

If the buffet table is a long one the stand could be flanked by small trees (see fig. 18) using some of the same flowers. If, for instance, the colouring is green and white the trees could be choisya foliage and white single daisy heads, or even roses. The alternative is to use candlesticks with candle cups (see figs 8, 9 and 10) which might be filled with massed sweet peas and grey foliage, or cascades of clematis, or simply mixed foliage. The permutations are endless!

Marquees

As a professional florist I have over the years been employed to decorate every kind of marquee, from those which are no more than depressing tents to those which are beautifully lined and lighted. Where there is a coloured lining thought should be given to the colouring available in the garden. Sometimes the marquee embraces a large flower bed or a big central urn filled with flowering plants, in which case the lining should be chosen to match the predominant colours of the bed or urn. I have seen linings which clashed horribly with flower beds. One marquee had a rather crude bright pink lining surrounding urns planted with orange South African marigolds, deep blue lobelias and red salvias.

I once worked in a marquee which enclosed a rose garden, a stone balustrade and steps. The roses were all in shades of white, cream and gold, and the marquee was lined with gold material which looked like silk. In this particular case the marquee was used as the sitting-out area for a coming-of-age dance. There were no central poles, but a rod ran the whole length of the roof. We obtained large white plastic foundations which would normally be used for hanging baskets. Instead of filling them with soil we lined them with polythene to retain moisture and filled them with Oasis bricks enclosed in polythene bags. If Oasis is not in polythene it will very quickly dry out and the flowers will droop. We filled the baskets with grey helichrysum mixed with variegated foliage, long sprays of yellow and white roses and philadelphus stripped of all its leaves. When completed the baskets were about three feet across. Small occasional tables were covered with yellow muslin cloths, and in the middle of each table stood a small wicker basket filled with tiny variegated ivies and white marguerites. The decorations were of course in this case on a very grand scale, but an equally pretty scheme could be achieved on a much smaller scale. For instance, instead of the hanging baskets containing fresh flowers and foliage they could be filled with plants. Afterwards they could be used as hanging baskets for a patio garden, or the plants could be transferred to tubs.

Marquees are most often used for wedding receptions, dances and cocktail parties. Very soon the space, which at first seems to be dauntingly large, becomes filled with people standing, so any flower decorations should be high up. If there are poles they make ideal spots from which to hang flowers. Sometimes the poles are covered with the same material used for the lining of the marquee, but this covering can be drawn aside to allow nails to be hammered into the poles. If two nails are driven in, one on each side of the pole, large blocks of Oasis encased in polythene bags and chicken wire can be hooked onto it and used as the foundation for large flowing flower arrangements carrying out the colours of the lining (see fig. 16). I often finish off such decorations with long ribbon streamers mounted onto wire and pushed into the Oasis (see fig. 17).

If the occasion is a wedding reception the table for the cake makes a good focal point. Fig. 18 shows a round table covered with muslin decorated by garlands of ivy, with the cake in the centre and two 'trees' on either side. The 'trees' stand in large flower pots filled with earth into which have been pushed

17 A ribbon streamer

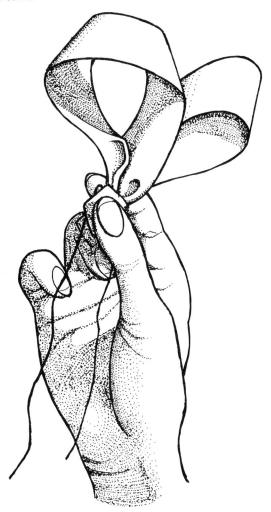

broom handles cut to the required length. A wet block of Oasis encased in a polythene bag and chicken wire is pressed on to the top of the handle (see fig. 19). The base of the cake is surrounded by Victorian posies of small dried flowers encircled by 'lace' frills which are in fact quite good plastic imitations! In the example illustrated choisya foliage, white daisies and kumquat fruits were used to create the tops of the trees. There are many other types of foliage and flowers which are equally suitable.

Smaller trees could be made for the buffet table described on page 117, and would be equally effective for a reception in a marquee. Small flower pots are used for the little trees on the buffet table. Dowelling is used instead of broom

handles and the pot is filled with plaster of Paris into which the dowelling 'trunk' is placed and held in position until the plaster has set. The top of the dowelling holds a small piece of Oasis, and the 'tree' is made in exactly the same way as the large trees described above.

Pedestals

There are many special occasions when it is necessary to have flowers at a height: vases low down on tables or chests will be lost the moment the room becomes filled with guests. It is far better to have one or two large groups at strategic points than several small arrangements scattered about. This is where the pedestal is so useful. Pedestals come in many types and many sizes. The most practical, because they blend in naturally with most backgrounds, are those made in black wrought iron, with a top which can be adjusted to be fixed at different heights as required, and the wooden variety. I have a pair of splendid converted mahogany bedposts, about five and a half feet high (and so only suitable for very high rooms), but I also have odd plant stands with nice

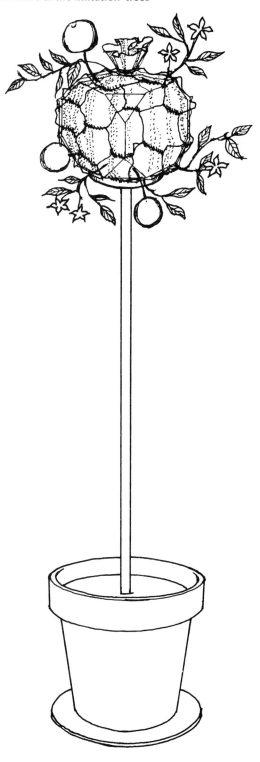

flat tops on which to place large bowls of flowers, and some smaller wooden pedestals. It is still possible to find suitable stands in antique and junk shops.

There are many white-painted iron pedestals about and these are fine if placed against a light wall; but they look horrible against dark papered or panelled walls. A pedestal should merge into the background unless it is particularly beautiful and in keeping with the rest of the furnishings.

I have a workbox which never has any sewing materials inside because it has a pedestal shape which makes it perfect for special flowers. I open the lid and insert a bowl in which the flowers are arranged (see colour pl. 7). The open lid makes a good background for light-coloured flowers. The photograph shows how well white and cream flowers show up against the dark wood.

Nowadays there are many skilled flower arrangers with original ideas, and the standard gets better and better. There is, however, one area of decorating in which all confidence seems to be undermined, and that is the pedestal arrangement. People who have filled their houses and churches with beautiful groups become panic-stricken at the prospect of arranging a large vase on a pedestal. I find that when several of my friends are combining to help to arrange the flowers for a wedding or a dance the pedestals are often left to me – quite unnecessarily!

Pedestal vases take a lot of material. Asked to do a pedestal arrangement I am told: 'There will be wonderful flowers and foliage for you, all ready and conditioned.' Not always true, I fear. I have sometimes been confronted by a tiny half-empty bucket with nothing in it but a few mauve and pink pyrethrums, some sad roses and a lot of heavy green – not the most inspiring collection!

When planning a vase on a pedestal remember that it has to be seen at a distance, so it should include material which will form a strong outline, but not a heavy one, some good big leaves and flowers to make a focal point. This is a term that always grates because it sounds so contrived; but it is important in the case of large arrangements to have a focal point or, to put it another way, a 'face' to the vase. The large leaves or flowers are placed to provide this. The other material should look as if it springs from this face, not as if it had been planted as a window-box all along the edge! Make sure, therefore, when collecting material for a pedestal vase that it includes large leaves like those of hosta, mahonia or bergenia, for example, as well as interesting foliage. Try to choose some branches which bend to the right and others to the left: so often they all bend the same way. If possible select flowers of different shapes, some pointed, like delphiniums and foxgloves, some with good rounded heads, like paeonies, roses such as 'Grandpa Dickson', and, later in the season, hydrangea. Flowering shrubs are very helpful – philadelphus, wiegela, osmanthus, for example – placed so that they cascade over the front and sides, preventing the vase from being too stiff. Vinca and ivies also help in this way. I am not, of course, suggesting that these will all be available at the same time, but merely indicating the type of material for which to aim.

When the material has been collected and conditioned put it on a dustsheet keeping the different types and colours together. If there are to be two pedestals, divide the material in two, making sure that there are right-facing branches for the right-hand pedestal and left-facing branches for the left-hand pedestal. It is so easy to finish one pedestal and then find that the other one has been left bereft of suitable material. Do make sure that the mechanics (see page 105) are firmly secured in the container. Heavy material can easily topple over if the chicken wire is not adequate and properly fixed. For pedestal vases I use large green washing-up bowls, or old-fashioned wash-stand basins – any container in fact which is wide and fairly deep. Once the flowers are arranged the bowl is not seen, so it is only the size and shape which matter.

Cones (see page 106) are often necessary as there may not be enough tall flowers. Cones may be filled with heavy branches and need to be pushed well into the chicken wire so that they do not slip about. I sometimes put a heavy branch in a central position at the back of the container and pushed deep down to the bottom of it. This makes a firm foundation on to which cones can be wired. Fill the cones with water and top them up when the arrangement is complete; and remember each day as you fill up the vase also to fill up the cones.

My feeling is that a pedestal vase should not end up looking like a stiff and unnatural triangle. To avoid a flat effect you should as you fill the container put one stem so that it comes forward, the next so that it goes backward, the next recessed low down and so on. Fill in the outline and general shape, including lots of cascading and arching material both at the front and at the sides, and leave a space in the middle. The focal point should then be completed – if this is done at the beginning it is very hard to place the other material – and you should then stand back a long distance from the vase to check the effect. There may be gaps which need to be filled. Make sure that the whole arrangement is well balanced and sitting right down on to the pedestal so that it makes a complete picture. Sometimes the flowers and the pedestal look like two separate entities!

Make sure that the back of the container is filled in: it may be seen from an angle. Then fill up the container and the cones with water and spray in particular any large leaves.

As I say endlessly to flower classes, 'If the mechanics are right anyone can arrange a pedestal vase'. It is, however, very hard to judge the exact quantities that you need for a large arrangement. It depends on size, position, lighting, and the type of material available. It may therefore be helpful to give some guidance both on quantities and on suitable material for a large vase on a pedestal.

Quantities

Foliage: about ten branches, some bending to the right and some to the left. Try to include different shades of green as well as variegated.

Flowering shrubs: about ten stems, some arching and some upright or

Berried shrubs: about ten stems. These will be more readily available in the autumn, when the flowering shrubs are over.

Large leaves: at least seven.

Flowers: if the vase includes flowering shrubs or berries, about 25 stems. If berries and shrubs are not available, about 36 stems for a large pedestal arrangement.

Material

The following material is particularly suited to pedestal arrangements because it lasts well and gives variety of form and texture.

Foliage: camellia, choisya, eleagnus, euonymus, hedera (ivy), ligustrum (privet), mahonia, pittosporum, ruta, *Weigela variegata*.

Leaves to use singly: bergenia, cardoon, fatsia, hosta, phormium, *Polygonatum multiflorum* (Solomon's seal).

Flowers with pointed tops: antirrhinum, campanula, delphinium, eremurus, gladiolus, larkspur, asters (Michaelmas daisies), nicotiana, pentstemon.

Flowers of more rounded form: alstroemeria, carnations, chrysanthemum, dahlia, daisies, *Helleborus foetidus*, lilies, paeonies, rudbeckia, sedum, zinnia.

Flowering shrubs: deutzia, escallonia, forsythia, fuchsia, hydrangea, lonicera (honeysuckle), osmanthus, philadelphus, prunus, rhododendron, ribes, roses, spiraea 'Bridal Wreath', syringa, *Viburnum opulus*, *Viburnum tinus*, weigela.

Berried shrubs: acuba, berberis, cotoneaster, *Euonymus europaeus* (spindle tree), ilex, *Mahonia aquifolium* (black), skimmia, symphoricarpus.

Constructions

There are occasions when it is helpful to use flowers or foliage to produce a solid mass of colour rising to a height either from floor level or from a table or shelf; for example, side tables in a ballroom or a large reception area. I have already suggested (see page 116) how a saucepan stand may be used for a buffet table decoration. A small construction can be used for the same purpose.

Any good handyman can easily make a construction. An upright of the required height is bolted to a base about 12 inches long and 9 inches wide. Flat wooden shelves, one above the other, are fixed at intervals up the upright, long enough and wide enough to hold oblong blocks of wet Oasis on their special trays. Another shelf is fixed to the top of the construction large enough to support a small container: a freezer bowl will do very well (fig. 20). A seed tray to hold more Oasis is placed on the base. The Oasis on the trays is enclosed in polythene bags, and, to give added support, the shelves are surrounded with chicken wire (see fig. 21).

Attach pieces of wire to bunches of grapes and tie them on to the chicken wire. Fix green peppers by pushing stub wires through them and into the Oasis.

20 The basis for a pyramid construction

21 The wooden shelves covered with chicken wire

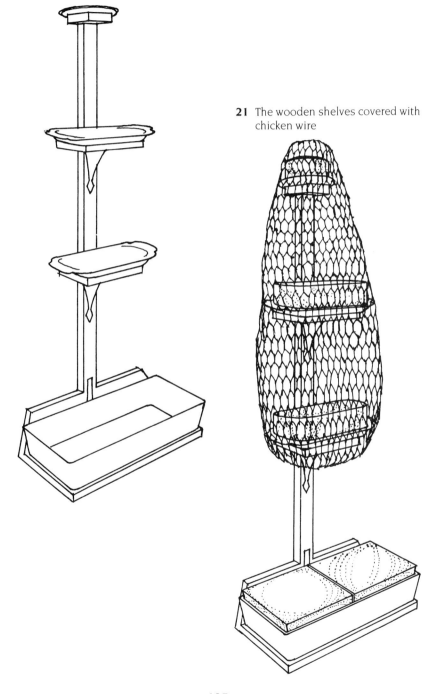

125

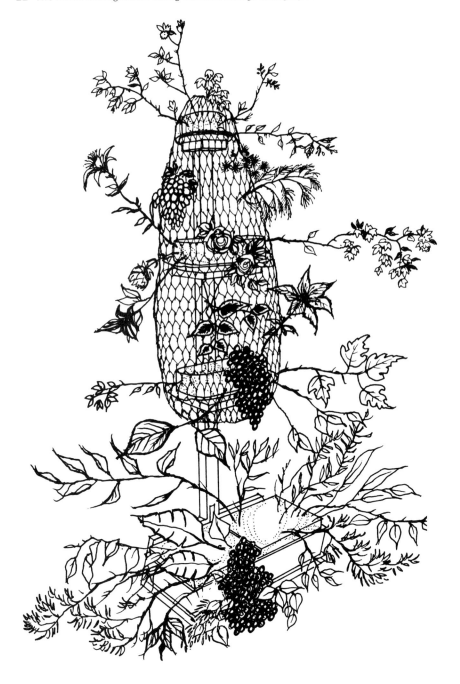

23 The completed arrangement

Use some of the material to make an outline and then fill it in (see fig. 22). Make sure that the Oasis in the seed box is always kept damp, and in hot weather spray the construction at least twice a day.

I used a series of these constructions, made entirely of foliage, peppers and grapes, when decorating a ballroom for a coming-out dance. They sat on marble-topped commodes and made impressive banks of green down one side of the room. The construction in fig. 23 sits on a side table and was used in an entrance hall for a special party.

Church flowers

Of the events where flowers play an important part perhaps the most obvious are weddings and other special occasions in church, but as I have dealt fully with these in my book *Flower Arranging and Flower Festivals in Church* I intend to give here only some very general guidelines.

The very size of the building presents a particular problem whether you are simply 'doing the flowers' for an ordinary Sunday or whether the occasion is a special one. At all times flowers should be so placed that they will immediately be seen. It is a good idea to have an arrangement in the porch, or just inside the door, and to try to lead the eye from there up to the chancel, bearing in mind that when flowers have to be seen at a distance it is better to have a few large arrangements, containing some sizeable flowers and good big leaves like those of *Hosta sieboldiana* and cardoon, rather than to have a number of small ones.

Pedestals and constructions, which I have referred to on pages 120 and 124 respectively, are invaluable, because they lift the flowers to eye-level. Churches give plenty of scope for the use of garlands. Garlands are very pretty encircling the tops of pillars, festooned in front of choir stalls, and outlining the door of the porch. They can be designed to fit in with the general colour-scheme of the building; alternatively, they can be made entirely of mixed foliage and also, in season, of alchemilla and cow parsley.

Most churches contain bright colour, in windows and elsewhere, and flowers can often be used effectively to pick up the colours of the building. It is, however, important to have regard to lighting and to bear in mind that some colours, particularly blue and mauve, will be lost against certain backgrounds.

I have referred to the size of the building, but this should not alarm the ordinary arranger on the rota with a small garden. Even a little garden should be able to provide enough material for the occasional vase in church, and, if flowers are in short supply, different foliages can be very effectively used.

8. Christmas decorations

I love Christmas and I find it sad that some people think of it as 'a bore' and would like to get away from it all. We have been fortunate in always spending it at home and seeing more family and friends than at any other time of the year. This makes it a splendid excuse for fairly extensive decorating. Our home is an old country cottage so we base our decoration on a foundation of evergreens from the garden, like camellia, skimmia and choisya, together with holly – augmented by the gold and silver variegated kinds from a generous friend – and armfuls of berried ivy. Fir cones are collected whenever possible and stored away for Christmas. In early December I take the seed heads that have been put aside in autumn and I either paint them gold or silver or dip them in glitter. I also add glitter to some of the ivy and I occasionally paint one or two leaves – not too much, otherwise they look like plastic. Lots of red ribbon and candles and those little Christmas tree baubles make up the rest. It is far better to limit the colours throughout the house rather than have a mass of different ones. Red, green and gold, silver and blue, and green and silver all show up well against winter foliage.

We always hope that the Christmas rose, *Helleborus niger*, will make the Christmas table centre. Unfortunately, it is usually about two weeks too late: but there is *Jasminum nudiflorum*. Those lovely yellow star-like flowers are at their best then. *Prunus autumnalis*, too, often flowers profusely at this time; a few branches of that magical shrub is a decoration in itself. If it is not sufficiently forward by the middle of December, cut branches and force them in warm water. If holly has to be cut in advance, simply leave it out on the lawn and bring it in when you are ready to use it.

When the children were small I was very disorganized. I used to tear about at the last minute putting decorations wherever space permitted with no thought or scheme in mind. This resulted in a hotch-potch of wholly unrelated decorating and extreme bad temper. Now I plan in advance and greatly enjoy the whole affair.

Decide well in advance where the decorations are to go. It is far better to have one or two stunning groups than several unrelated vases. Family and friends should be welcomed from the start. What better place than the front door and the hall? A wreath of evergreens is easily made to hang from the door knocker. Most florists sell the round metal foundations used for funeral work. Tie small plastic bags filled with wet Oasis round the foundation with garden string and push in sprays of holly and mixed greenery. Put fir cones on to stub wires and push them in at intervals. Finish off with a large ribbon bow. The alternative is to take a large potato and cut off a slice at the back so that it will hang flat against the door. Take a 12 inch stub wire and make a hook at one end. Pull the wire right through leaving the hooked end at the bottom, which will secure it. Attach the other end round the knocker and hide it with ribbon. Cut small sprays of holly, box, cupressus or any other lasting greenery and push them into the potato. The overall shape can be oval, elongated or whatever you prefer. I personally like to put in two or three trailing stems of variegated holly. Finish off with a large bow.

A large house may have space on either side of the front door for the mock standard trees described on page 117. At Christmas these can be made of holly with ribbon bows. If more colour is required, Christmas tree baubles are effective. Simply attach them to shortened stub wires and push them into the greenery. They replace the kumquats shown in fig. 19.

The hall is an important area and very often makes the ideal setting for a Christmas tree. Most families have over the years collected various decorations for the tree, but if you are starting afresh limit the baubles to one or two colours and tie them to the branches with small ribbon bows. Fortunately, the old fragile variety has been replaced by one which is unbreakable, so it is worth while buying an interesting collection. There are very effective transparent balls giving the effect of huge raindrops and rather pretty hanging icicles. A tree decorated only with these has a fairy-like appearance.

In most houses the staircase is in a central position and makes an attractive background. We hang from the newel post a decoration of which the foundation is a large block of wet Oasis in a plastic bag encased with chicken wire. Into it are pushed sprays of berried ivy, variegated foliage and holly. Ivy trails are looped up the banisters at intervals (see fig. 24). In the case of a large house with a long winding staircase blocks of Oasis can be lashed on at intervals and the pattern repeated. Be warned: a surprising amount of greenery is needed.

Over the Christmas period there are always visitors coming and going, including small children eager to investigate anything new, so I suggest that in the drawing-room all decorations should be kept high up. We fit a large container into the top of a china cabinet and fill it with evergreens and as much winter jasmine as possible mixed with variegated holly which spills over the front and sides. I attach to some of the branches golden baubles, using them as 'flowers', and painted fir cones.

24 A decorated staircase

The chestnut roaster is used once more, but this time filled with holly and ivy.

The dining-room is the most important room: after all, lunch or dinner is the highlight of a family Christmas Day, and later there is New Year's Eve. If the autumn has been warm there may be enough hellebores to mix with ivy leaves: they make the perfect table centre. Unfortunately, this seldom happens in our part of the world. This year, however, we did have late red garden roses which we had in candle cups (see page 107) with sprays of euonymus, ivy and holly spilling over the sides. In the centre of the table a Wedgewood leaf plate was filled with fruit and gourds forming a tall pyramid. Red Christmas baubles were tucked in with walnuts and ivy leaves painted gold. Another good idea for table decorations is to have the small trees described on page 119, made on this occasion from holly and ivy and finished with small ribbon bows. They are particularly useful for those with no access to gardens, because they use very little green. Useful too is the 'tree' of honesty and everlasting flowers mentioned on page 64; it is transformed into a Christmas decoration by attaching to its branches small silver baubles with toffees in silver and red shiny paper hanging below. These gradually diminish when our grandchildren are staying, but the tree still looks very pretty reflected in the looking-glass behind. Many people living in flats or small town houses will have very little greenery available. They should find candle cups on tall candlesticks particularly useful. Trails of mixed variegated and light-coloured evergreen foliage springing from a central coloured candle make easy and economical decorations and are Christmassy and pretty.

Bibliography

CHATTO, Beth, *Plant Portraits*, in association with the Daily Telegraph Sunday Magazine

EVISON, Raymond, J., *Making the Most of Clematis*, Flora Print

FISH, Marjorie, *Gardening in the Shade*, Faber

HAY, Roy and SYNGE, Patrick H., *The Dictionary of Garden Plants*, in collaboration with the RHS

HELLYER, Arthur, *The Garden Adviser*, Macdonald

LLOYD, Christopher, *Foliage Plants*, Viking

MACQUEEN, Sheila, *Complete Flower Arranging*, Hyperion

MANN, Pauline, *Flowers that Last: Arranging Dried and Preserved Flowers*, Batsford

MILLAR, Gault, *The Dictionary of Shrubs in Colour*, in collaboration with RHS handbooks

PEARSON, Robert, *Patio Gardening*, Hamlyn paperbacks

Fred Whitsey's Garden Calendar, in association with the Daily Telegraph

All Wisley Handbooks especially *Lilies*, *Groundcover*, *Annuals & Biennials*, RHS

It is impossible to list every nursery in Great Britain that I recommend for specific plants. However, *The Plant Finder*, published by the Hardy Plant Society, lists where to buy over 22,000 plants.

Index